THE
HORIZONTAL
WORLD

THE

HORIZONTAL WORLD

growing up wild
in the middle of nowhere

DEBRA MARQUART

COUNTERPOINT
A MEMBER OF THE PERSEUS BOOKS GROUP
NEW YORK

Published by Counterpoint,
A Member of the Perseus Books Group

Counterpoint books are available at special discounts for bulk
purchases in the United States by corporations, institutions,
and other organizations. For more information, please contact
the Special Markets Department at the Perseus Books Group,
11 Cambridge Center, Cambridge MA 02142, or call
(617) 252-5298 or (800) 255-1514, or e-mail
special.markets@perseusbooks.com.

Library of Congress Cataloging-in-Publication Data
Marquart, Debra K.
The horizontal world : growing up wild in the middle of
nowhere / Debra Marquart.
p. cm.
ISBN-13: 978-1-58243-345-5 (hardcover : alk. paper)
ISBN-10: 1-58243-345-3 (hardcover : alk. paper) 1. Marquart,
Debra K.—Childhood and youth. 2. Marquart, Debra K.—
Homes and haunts—North Dakota. 3. Authors, American—
Homes and haunts—North Dakota. 4. Authors, American—
20th century—Biography. 5. North Dakota—Social life and
customs. I. Title.
PS3563.A7112Z465 2006
811'.54—dc22
2005028218

06 07 08 09/ 10 9 8 7 6 5 4 3 2 1

In memory of my father and for my mother

*He thought of all his years away from home, the years of
wandering in many lands and cities. He remembered how
many times he had thought of home with such an intensity of
passion that he could close his eyes and see the scheme of
every street, and every house upon every street, and the faces of
the people, as well as recall the countless things that they had
said and the densely-woven fabric of all their histories. . . .*

*But why had he always felt so strongly the magnetic pull of
home, why had he thought so much about it and remembered
it with such blazing accuracy, if it did not matter, and if this
little town, and the immortal hills around it, was not the only
home he had on earth? He did not know. All that he knew
was that the years flow by like water, and that one day men
come home again.*

—Thomas Wolfe, *You Can't Go Home Again*

CONTENTS

Prologue: Pilgrim Soul, xi

1 Things Not Seen in a Rearview Mirror, 1

2 The Land Husband, 27

3 The Most Famous Person from North Dakota, 53

4 Prodigal Daughters, 73

5 The Horizontal Life, 97

6 On Lost and Crazy Sisters, 119

7 Between Earth and Sky, 137

8 Great Falls, 159

9 To Kill a Deer, 177

10 Failures of the Heart, 205

11 Signs and Wonders, 227

Epilogue: Sustainable Agriculture:
The Farmer's Daughter Revisited, 253
Acknowledgments, 265
Works Cited, 269

PROLOGUE:
PILGRIM SOUL

Farmboys. How we avoided them when they came around, their hands heavy with horniness, their bodies thick with longing. *Be careful of farmboys,* we warned each other. *They know how to plant seeds.*

And who could say where their hands had been? On pitchforks, mowers, inside swathers, combines. They were patient boys, those long hours in the saddle of the tractor, plowing dark furrows in the fertile earth. They might be grasping the teats of milk cows at sunrise, killing gophers in the afternoon, and be on you by nightfall. No, no. Best to stick with townboys, their soft saliva mouths, their round corduroy shoulders, their talk of plans for college.

We were farmgirls running tall through pastures. We had long shiny hair and peach-fresh skin. Born to carry the milk bucket, the alfalfa bale, our hands soon mastered the manual transmission. We learned to speed shift, double clutch. Our feet never knew the brake. We roared down the section lines in our fathers' pickups, empty gas cans clanging in the truck bed. We left trails of dust behind us.

This was no little house on the prairie. We smeared musky blue shadow on our eyelids and raspberry gloss on our lips.

We wore platform shoes and bell-bottom jeans. It was the times. We were hip-huggered, and tight-sweatered, and navel-exposed. We walked around town like the James gang, tossing this and flashing that.

We came in pairs sometimes, first cousins, second cousins, double cousins—it thrilled the imagination. Some were brunette with delicate features, some had hair that hung heavy as gold down the angle of a jaw line. Some of us had wild laughs that never led to wild actions. Some had older sisters who got in trouble and had to get married or had to be sent away to homes for wayward girls.

We had strong white teeth. We shone them on the world. We spoke the international language of beauty. All the immigrant grandparents gossiped in German about us. We were wayward girls looking for the untroubled way. We were best in show, the pick of the litter, the cream of the crop, too good for this place, everyone agreed. We were programmed for flight.

We farmgirls lived north, south, east, and west of town. In the middle of all this was me—the girl that I was then—the watcher, leaning toward the periphery.

Grow Where You're Planted, that poster I had on my bedroom wall as a teenager, I know I never believed it. Was it the image I liked that made me duct-tape it to the wall? A daisy with a bent stalk growing out of a square pot. Two other posters, *Label Jars, Not People* and *Make Love, Not War*, I believed. But *Grow Where You're Planted*, never. In my childhood, like those people with suitcases packed and waiting for the mother ship, I prepared myself for transplantation.

Napoleon, the small town in North Dakota where I grew up—1,107 people, three bars, two grain elevators, a post office, a drugstore, a courthouse, a funeral home, and farmland stretching for miles in all directions. The only jobs I saw around me were farmer, banker, and priest. The prospects for women were worse—teacher, housewife, nun. Not one of them an occupation I imagined for myself.

I watched television for clues, *The Mary Tyler Moore Show,* about a beautiful single girl who twirled around and flung her hat in the air in a public square, she was so happy to be young and living in Minneapolis. She worked in a news office. That could be me. I watched *That Girl,* about a pretty single girl living in New York. She had a boyfriend, Ted, who came around almost every day. Her father lived nearby; she saw him occasionally.

I watched *A Family Affair,* a show about a teenage girl, Cissy, and two freckle-faced, strawberry blond kids, Buffy and Jody, whose parents had died in some way that we are never told. The program is a sitcom, and it would be too sad to know how the children were orphaned. They are sent to stay with their only living relative, their Uncle Bill, a city-dwelling bachelor played by the actor Brian Keith. It's unclear what he does for a living. He's far too busy and preoccupied to raise three needy children, and he is rich, rich, rich.

Fortunately, he has a butler, Mr. French, who is good with children, who can cook and clean and care for all their needs. The children warm to him. Mr. French is gentle and rotund and always ready with food. Each episode centers on the ways in which the two men are perplexed by the strange emotional world of the children who have been put in their charge.

Farmboys. Best to avoid them, with their forty head of Angus cattle, their prize bulls for breeding, their 160 acres of wheat.

A few years ago in the state of North Dakota during a campaign to raise money for family farms, the state tourism bureau produced a calendar of hunk bachelor farmers—gorgeous, four-color photographs—one shirtless bachelor farmer for every month of the year. They came in all varieties and sizes. They were big-armed, muscular, and deep-tanned, or they were small, well-toned, and scrappy, but they were all, each one of them, the calendar assured us, extremely lonely for women out there on the plains.

The same year, an article in the *Wall Street Journal* reported that multitudes of dairy farmers lived the same lonely life on the rolling, lake-pocked ranges in Minnesota. The article asked where all the big Minnesota farmgirls had gone? The answer: to the big Minnesota towns like St. Paul and Minneapolis.

Sustainable agriculture. Farmboys stay with the land; farmgirls run away to college, or to good jobs in the city. The *Journal* article reported that the lonely hunk dairy farmers were looking for wives, just as in the movie *Seven Brides for Seven Brothers.*

The state flower of North Dakota is the wild prairie rose, almost a desert flower. It crops up along roadsides and ditches, draws little attention to itself—prickly green foliage, tiny pink blossom bent low to the ground. A wallflower rose, I thought, for a wallflower state.

Called the "Roughrider State"—after Theodore Roosevelt's first U.S. Volunteer Cavalry, which actually fought dismounted in Cuba due to logistical problems—or the "Peace Garden State," after the Peace Gardens, North Dakota is also known as the "Flickertail State," a nickname inspired by the flicking of a running ground squirrel's tail.

Despite the abundance of Richardson's ground squirrel in North Dakota, legislation making it the state animal was defeated in 1953. That distinction now goes to the state's honorary equine, the Nokota horse, a unique breed thought to be a descendant of Sitting Bull's war ponies. The state drink of North Dakota is milk; the state dance is not the waltz, not the two-step, the polka or the rhumba, but the square dance.

In North Dakota, we had very little spring and even less fall. Three blistering months of summer packed between eight bitter months of winter. A season of blowing dirt followed by a season of snow and ice. And always there was the wind.

With sixteen inches of precipitation on the hundredth meridian, even less in the western parts of the state, only the toughest grasses survive: buffalo and gramma grasses, little bluestem, switchgrass, crested wheatgrass. Even fields of sweet corn can't reach full maturity in the short growing season. Farmers grow the hardiest crops—flax, barley, sunflowers, Marquis hard red spring or durum wheat, introduced from Russia for its ability to ripen early.

Drive through the plains states west of the hundredth meridian in summer, and you will see the fields shot through with crops of gold and yellow and tan. Fewer crops of deep, verdant green like the corn and soybeans that prosper in wetter states like Iowa and Illinois. Plants that grow west of the hundredth meridian must learn to survive on less or die.

Sometimes towngirls who don't know any better marry farmboys. First, they get all soft and romantic at the sight of those rugged farmboy hands. Then they begin to imagine their idyllic life on the farm. *It would be nice to have some animals,* the towngirls croon. *Maybe a horse or two.*

It's a farmgirl code not to warn the towngirls about the farmboys, about their horny hands and their uncanny ability to plant seeds. It's retribution, a farmgirl payback.

Towngirls had noon lunches at home, while farmgirls sat on hard school benches eating not-so-hot hot lunches. Towngirls got to be cheerleaders, school newspaper editors, homecoming queens.

Farmgirls got to milk cows, haul bales, pick rocks. They got to work in the barns and the fields beside their brothers, the farmboys, like equals in the cold winters and hot summers.

Each year on the last day of school, the farmgirls mounted the steaming row of buses on the curb for the long ride home. They were going far from town now—east, west, north, south—sometimes hour-long bus rides deep into the country.

Goodbye, farmgirls. The towngirls rode by on their banana bikes and waved, not in a mean way, but in a towngirl way, oblivious to any hardship around them. *See you in three months,* the towngirls sang, thinking about a long summer of picnics and swimming-pool afternoons.

The farmgirls glowered at the towngirls through the bus windows, thinking of spreading straw with pitchforks when they got home. The farmgirls knew that in the summer, aside from church, they might get to town three or four times: a few Friday nights, the Corn Show, maybe the Fourth of July. By the end of the summer, they knew their boyfriends would be towngirl boyfriends.

Now it was rude awakening time for the towngirls. It's best they not know what's coming. *Someone has to stay with the land,* the farmgirls think, *and it better not be us.* Soon enough it will be towngirl hands weeding the acres of carrots and potatoes.

Some of the towngirls take to farm life, make the best of it. They throw themselves into gardening, canning. They get really good at it. They take up rosemaling. They buy old dressers and learn to strip and revarnish them. They dig antique clay pots out of junkyards and place them in their foyers as umbrella stands.

But many of the towngirls break under the pressure and run away from their tanned, muscular husbands, leaving behind toddlers and teenagers. Many farmboys get left behind like this, even the choicest ones, like those featured in the state tourism bureau's Hunk Bachelor Farmer calendar.

The farmhouse I grew up in was once an icehouse, a thick hull of four walls where ice was stored for people to buy in slab form before home refrigeration. People say my great-grandfather, Joseph Marquart, bought the icehouse from the creamery in town a few years after he immigrated to Dakota Territory from his village in south Russia. They say he hauled it with oxen across the lake that stands between our farm and town, during the coldest part of winter when the lake was completely frozen over.

He dragged the shell of the icehouse up the hill of our farm and set it on the basement foundation he had prepared. He added a second floor with many rooms for all his children and a balcony that ran around the exterior of the second floor. My older cousin Tony, who grew up in the house, told me that Great-Grandpa liked to sit on the balcony and look out over the many acres he owned. He liked to imagine the generations of his family that would live together in this place for many years to come.

It was a big, drafty farmhouse with creaky wood floors, one bathroom installed in the fifties, a large kitchen with a round table in the center, a coal furnace in the basement, and staircases steep as ladders.

The bedrooms were hot and airless in the summer, freezing in the winter. The windows blew like saxophones in the hard wind of Alberta clippers. Each day of the winter, I woke up cold in that icehouse, my red nose peeking out from under the blankets. I dreaded setting my bare foot down on the freezing wood floor. I knew some of my grandparents had died in those rooms.

Watching *A Family Affair* as a child, I coveted most the high-rise apartment that Buffy and Jody got to live in. The elevators were nice, I thought, as was the friendly doorman. The apartment's large windows overlooked the lights of the city, and Mr. French was always waiting with a tray of cookies.

I watched *The Bob Newhart Show*, about a mild-mannered psychologist working in downtown Chicago. I liked Bob Hartley's patient nature. All around, he was surrounded by strange, nervous people, but no problem presented by a client or a friend seemed too outrageous to him.

At night he went home to his beautiful wife Emily played by the actress Suzanne Pleshette, who had a deep voice and a horsey laugh. They cooked dinner together and talked about what kind of a day they'd had. They drank wine from fluted glasses and looked out over the lights of the city.

"You can't get there from here," my father used to say when I spoke too long or enthusiastically about the cities I planned to someday run away to. I had consulted maps; I thought I knew otherwise. Did he mean to imply that the gravel road outside our farm was not connected to other roads, and that those freeways had not been paved and multi-laned in preparation for my flight?

As a child, I remember my mother as overworked and preoccupied, slamming doors and cupboards. She was always busy with her hands, milking cows, washing dishes, canning, sewing, gardening, working with the farm bills, the messy pile of receipts, her worried fingers on the calculator. She was always running from place to place.

In the barn, she would throw a milker on the cow then run across the yard into the house to put dinner in the oven. From my upstairs teenage bedroom, where I was reading or listening to the radio, or playing my big Kay guitar with two squiggly *F*'s for sound holes, I might be singing spirituals or protest folk songs about suffering and endless hours of labor in the fields, and I would hear her fling the door open downstairs and then the house would shake with the stomping of her feet.

She'd throw open the refrigerator and tear the roast from its wrapper. She would clatter a pan on the kitchen counter then throw the roast in with a loud thump. She'd tear open the packet of French onion soup, sprinkle it over the meat, run a little tap water into the pan, throw the whole thing in the oven, and be out the door and back to the barn in time to take the milker off the finished cow and put it on the next one.

One day, my mother stopped at the foot of the stairs to listen to me. I didn't hear her come in. I was practicing my solo for choir, testing the limits of my voice.

"The Lord's Prayer," I remember I was singing. *For thine is the kingdom*—I was climbing to the crescendo—*and the power*—I was building to the climax—*and the glory*—approaching the rarefied atmosphere only the first soprano can inhabit—*for-e-ver*—I was holding and holding the second syllable, the high note—*for-e-ver*—I was stretching time, losing meter, my voice shaking the windows with its power, and before I could bring it down to the *Amen*, settle the song gently to the ground, I heard another voice break through, a louder voice, screaming from downstairs. I could barely make it out, the words *shut up* I heard, and my mother's voice screaming louder than I could sing—"Shut up"—and yelling up the stairs, "Don't sing in the house," my mother's voice yelling, "Just stop singing in the house."

What is the sound of a pilgrim soul singing? As a child growing up in North Dakota, I felt myself wanting to grow tall and wild. When you're young, it's natural to be green and vivid. But I heard cautions all around me: "You're not so hot"; "Don't get too big for your britches."

How to find sustenance and nurture oneself to maturity in a place that yields only sixteen inches of precipitation a year? Like the grasses and crops around us, we lived on the narrow margin of life. Large houses, shiny cars, nice clothes, big talk—all unnecessary expenditures of limited resources.

Best not to sprout unsustainable foliage. Then what will you do during the dry years? We watched each other for signs of vanity. Anyone inclined toward extravagance was pruned back, wing-clipped: "She's beautiful, but she knows it"; "He thinks his shit doesn't stink."

If I were a flower, I thought, I would want to be a hollyhock, a tall, sturdy stalk, opening large flowers everywhere, or a tiger lily, orange and black petals opening shamelessly to the world.

I knew the effects of drought, had witnessed it in my father's fields—stalks and sheaves withered on the vine. Nothing sadder than the nodding head of a dry bud.

Still I dared to imagine myself in full blossom. I could be the pampered rose, unbridled beauty accompanied by thorns, or the hothouse orchid, a fragile thing that everyone fusses over. Even in this dry place, I told myself, I must find a way to bloom. I must never allow myself to be blighted.

In 1974, my parents drove me to Bismarck, where I would be attending junior college, and dropped me off at the front door of my girls' dorm with my few boxes of clothes, records, and books. They didn't come up to my room. They were worried about rush hour traffic and getting home in time to do chores.

The goodbyes were not tearful. I was the youngest and wildest of their five children. I won't say they were glad to be rid of me. Perhaps they were just happy to be on their own for the first time in twenty-five years.

I suppose I stood on the front steps of the dorm and waved goodbye to them as they drove off, and I imagine they waved back. They were not the kind of people who didn't wave back.

The half-mile stretch of gravel road leading out of my parents' farm is framed on either side by cottonwood trees that are over seventy feet tall. My great-grandfather planted these trees, grown from a packet of government seeds given to prairie farmers, after he arrived from Russia in the 1880s.

In my 1960s childhood, I felt the cottonwoods loomed like giants over us, ringing the northern edge of our yard. I was frightened of their height. I had nightmares that the thick trunks would come down in the heavy wind; that they would fall the entire length of our big backyard, break through the roof, and crush me in my bed. I did not understand then about the deep tangle of roots underneath that holds things up, that holds things in place.

The day before I left home for college, I took a photograph of the road leading out of my parents' farm—the long driveway stretching out to the open wheat fields and the giant tops of the cottonwoods reaching up to the sky. The photograph must have been taken in late afternoon. The shadows are long. The light is cast in gold and bronze, the sweet color of memory.

The picture of home was one undeveloped frame in my camera, the first in a succession of images I planned to collect of more interesting places. I got myself on that road, and I did not wave back. I concentrated only on flight.

And for a long time, it seemed to me, North Dakota looked best only when glanced at briefly while adjusting the rearview mirror.

THINGS NOT SEEN
IN A REARVIEW MIRROR

On the morning of my father's funeral in 1996, a house on the road blocked for a time all flow of traffic on Highway 3, the two-lane blacktop in central North Dakota that stretches south of I–94 to my hometown. I spotted the house first as a sliver of roof and eaves weaving like an apparition on the horizon where the road should have been.

"Is that a house?" I asked my husband, who knows best to drive and remain quiet the closer we get to ground zero. We had driven six hundred miles the day before and collapsed into bed at a hotel in Jamestown, an hour away.

Highway 3 runs parallel to, and only a few miles shy of, the hundredth meridian. This north-south line of demarcation— described by Wallace Stegner in *Beyond the Hundredth Meridian* as "an inflexible line of aridity"—is generally considered to mark the end of the Midwest and the beginning of the West.

Beyond this point, precipitation drops to between eight and sixteen inches annually, and Stegner notes that twenty inches of precipitation a year is the minimum needed for unaided agriculture. Another forty miles west of here, the Missouri River crooks south, on its way to joining the Mississippi and eventually the Gulf of Mexico. In the end, water returns to water, leaving behind sagebrush, tumbleweed.

As early as the 1820s, Major Stephen Long's expedition to the Rocky Mountains deemed this part of the country inhospitable for life. His chronicler, Edwin James, cautioned that this region should "forever remain the unmolested haunt of the native hunter, the bison, and the jackal."

Here is the uncharted world into which Lewis and Clark took their famous voyage north and west two hundred years ago. Passing through this part of Dakota Territory on October 19, 1804, Captain Meriwether Lewis recorded in his journal seeing countless buffalo, elk, pelicans, white-tailed deer, and trumpeter swans. The expedition spotted herds of pronghorned antelope, which the explorers inaccurately identified as goats. In what is now North Dakota, they encountered their first grizzly bear.

They saw abandoned Arikara encampments and the high, strong watchtowers of a ruined Mandan village, as well as stone monuments and remarkable natural formations—high round hills that formed a core at the top where they spotted golden eagles nesting. On October 20 in this part of Dakota Territory, they encountered a pack of ten wolves. They wounded a white bear and discovered the tracks of an animal whose paw print was three times larger than the foot of a man.

Today as you travel west through North Dakota on I–94 toward Montana, you'll notice that slopes get deeper and roads get lonelier. West of the Missouri, towns get smaller and farther in between. Precipitation diminishes; population density decreases. Buildings look broken down, boarded up, and thirsty for paint. Whole towns consist of two bars, a post office, and a grain elevator. It's likely the only number on the rise in this part of the country is the percentage of guns and Bibles per capita.

There's room to grow strange and idiosyncratic here, room to spread out your power tools and abandon your rusted cars. But aside from the "Get US out of the UN" sign slathered in red paint on a sloping barn near Dawson (right next to the yellow "Honey for Sale!" sign), you would not sense anything unusual while driving Highway 3—just an endless succession of farms, fields, and fences.

On the morning of my father's funeral, I kept waiting for the next curve or rise to correct my vision, expecting the growing roof of the house on the road to slither to the right or left and become simply one more farmhouse on the side of the road.

I know the topography of this drive from every conceivable angle, could read it with my fingers like Braille. If you installed my memory like a slotted reel on a player piano, the ghostly keys would play out this tune: There is the gravel turnoff to Grandma and Grandpa Geist's old place; there's the farm where the Doll triplets lived; there's the ruin of the old country store where the little boy was run over by a milk truck. This is the place of dust where I spent my childhood, the place that extracted from me the price of one childhood.

On the morning of my father's funeral, as we came over the next rise, I saw we had three miles to go. This is Logan County. While it may be just another patch of flat horizon to someone driving through, to the people of my family it's the navel of the earth, the place from which all things flow and to which all things return in time.

A few miles up the highway is the hill where most of my family is buried—the Catholics, my father's side, in the graveyard east of the road, and my mother's family, the Lutherans, on the west side. My father would be buried on that hill later that morning, laid to rest within one mile of our farm, the place where he was born. This feels biblical to me, the full and eternal return, like the myth about Adam at Golgotha, buried in the very place where he was conceived.

Gravity seems to pull stronger in Logan County. I recall being conscious of it as a child, the grounding heaviness of the place. I imagined my life to be a held clock, a suspended pendulum that started ticking each time I laid my body down on the land. Whether to sleep or partake of the land's fruits, I knew I was binding myself to its earthly contracts. I tried to live lightly here, to move through this world as a slip or a shadow, to keep my appetites and desires to a minimum, lest I start the clock ticking in earnest.

As soon as possible, I moved away from Logan County, and I have lived in places where gravity pulls less on me—mostly college towns in other states. But no matter how far I travel, no matter how magnificent my flight, I fear this place will become jealous of my wandering and claim me as its own. By equally weird logic, I believe that if I avoid Logan County, death will have more trouble locating me.

"Please," I beg my husband at times when I feel really desperate. "If I ever get sick, no matter what happens to me, please don't send me home to die." I say this as a joke, so it doesn't sound demented.

It's usually in the middle of the night when I can't sleep, and I'm usually crying when I say it. I have woken him up to tell him all the things I'm concerned about. And when I get to this part—don't send me home to die—we usually both start laughing, it sounds so ridiculous to our ears.

But we laugh for different reasons. He laughs because he doesn't have a hillside in North America where all the bones of his ancestors are collected, and I laugh because no matter how far I wander, I know that hillside waits for me.

In front of us that morning stretched the low-lying bowl of land that once belonged to my great-grandfather, Joseph Marquart. He was born near the Black Sea in south Russia in 1856, one hundred years before me, and he died a wealthy man in central North Dakota in 1937. The headline of his obituary described him as the "Logan County Wheat King for a Quarter Century."

This is big: to be king of wheat in a part of the country where wheat is king. In my own time, I was Dairy Princess of Logan County, a short-lived title I was stripped of when I refused to attend the State Dairy Princess competition and pit my creamy milk maid thighs and flashing farmer's daughter eyes against those of beauties from across the state.

How many times had I asked my father to recount for me the number of sections of land Great-Grandpa had owned? And he'd stare in the air to the right, the place where all his memories seemed to be stored, and he'd tick them off on his fingers—the north fields, the south fields, the slough land, the lake acres, the gravel pit, the quarters by the wild woods— nine full sections of land, 5,760 acres, not counting the lots he owned in town, the land in western North Dakota, and the land in Saskatchewan he bought during his salad days.

In the early 1900s, within fifteen years of my great-grandfather's arrival in America, he had managed to acquire almost six thousand acres of land. How he accomplished this is unknown. When I've asked questions of some of the oldest people in town, I've been told that he was a good farmer, a shrewd horse trader, and that he had the immigrant's twin gift of enterprise and frugality.

In the early days of gasoline tractors, he devised a small tank on wheels with a nozzle that allowed him to travel by horse and cart from farm to farm and sell fuel. This was a rumor in our family until my brother unearthed the very tank with wheels in the dump ground near the lake that borders our land. The water was high that year, and when it receded, the rusty belly emerged after decades of burial.

In other popular stories, my great-grandfather was a rum runner during prohibition, bringing alcohol across the border from Canada. He was also reputed to have owned shares in a Colorado gold mine. He purchased the shares, supposedly, when he received remuneration from the French government for iron ore mines that his own grandparents had owned in Alsace. This story, impossible to verify, was set aside as fabrication until I learned that his nickname was Iron Joe—a vital clue, given that nicknames in my ethnic group are deep indicators of family trades.

In the only picture I have of my great-grandfather, he's sitting on a wooden bench in front of an old storefront. The picture was taken in the 1930s, near the end of his life. He's wearing a trim black suit and a brimmed hat. The image is grainy and has been copied many times. It's hard to make out the features of his face because he's wearing glasses and has a thick mustache. His hat brim is pulled down over his face making him look like someone in disguise, and perhaps he is.

The story in our family is that Joseph removed the letter *d* from our last name, Marquardt, when he came through Ellis Island in order to confuse the Russian military, which had forcibly conscripted him in 1882, and from which he was on the run in 1885 when he immigrated to America.

From the photo, it's possible to see his boldness even in old age. He's aimed his body into the lens. He's straightened his back and stilled himself for the camera's snap. Something in the set of his jaw says, "Posterity," as if he knows about the fact of me—that I, a person of his blood, will be here eighty years later staring back at him.

He looks relaxed, as if all real work in life has been done, and he's just in town on a sunny day with all the other old farmers to complain about wheat prices, shipping costs, and the lack of rain. His legs are set wide; his hands rest confidently on his thighs. Against the backdrop of his black trousers, his hands look massive, his fingers thick as sausages, his fists huge as ham hocks. Surely, this is an optical illusion. Taken in context, his hands appear larger than his face or his thin neck. They look brutish, as if they have grasped for much in life, growing more enormous with each acquisition. *These are the hands,* I think, *that got us out of Russia.*

What must it have been like for him, an immigrant, to come across this small ridge north of town on Highway 3 in the second half of his life and know that everything in sight belonged to him, had been shaped by his hand and the hands of children of his blood?

Before he died at the age of eighty, my great-grandfather distributed his wealth by setting off in severalty a parcel to each of his nine children, his obituary in the *Napoleon Homestead* reported, in appreciation of their cooperation. This description makes him sound kind of baronial—dispatching his land in parcels, as if ermine capes, rolls of parchment, and hot wax seals were involved.

In the 1930s, my own grandfather, Joseph, the namesake and eldest son, took over the heart of the farm, the land with the lake, the orchard, the original farmstead, and these low-lying fields surrounding it.

And in the 1950s, my father, Felix—who did not have the temperament to be a farmer, who had no aptitude with machinery, no affinity for livestock, who was impatient with nature, and believed he could will it to deliver sun or rain if he just got angry enough or stared out the window at it long enough—took over this farm and the lifetime of hard work, worry, and frustration that went with it, just so the land would not go out of the family.

In the end, my father fulfilled his generation's part of the agreement. On the morning of his funeral, I could look around and see the evidence: A mile ahead and to the right was the nest of white buildings on a gentle hill at the center of what was now my brother Nick's farm.

It was early June. The land spread out flat for miles. The grass in the pastures was lush. The fields lay in rich black furrows. The seeds buried deep were just cracking their husks and letting go of tender green shoots. We were close to home now. If not for the small rise on the northern edge of town, I would have been able to see the grain elevators jutting into the sky and the thin spire of the Catholic Church bell tower, which would be ringing, in moments, for my father.

The funeral would be at 10:00, but the rosary vigil began at 9:00. It was now 9:15. I imagined my distraught mother at the funeral chapel, clutching a ragged Kleenex, her nose red from crying. She would be sitting in the front pew as mourners passed by to view my father stretched out in his coffin. My brother and his wife, all my sisters and their husbands, and all the grandchildren would have arrived by now. "But where is Debbie," my mother would be wondering. "Has she been killed in a car accident?" My mother is a woman who believes in multipart tragedies, in life unraveling in complex and ironic ways, and as her youngest daughter, I have given her much grist for her worry mill.

If we had encountered this magnificent house on the road on any other stretch of Highway 3, we could have pulled out of the lane, hung in the ditch at a fierce angle, and stared in wonder for a few moments as it passed by, going north in the other lane. But on that day, we came upon the house precisely on the spot where county workers had decided, that anonymous morning, to repair a forty-foot stretch of the road. Workers in orange vests shoveled and packed down the soft tar. The right lane was cordoned off with a line of orange reflector cones.

My husband pulled our van onto the gravel shoulder and we joined a growing column of cars. Down the road, on the south side of the tarred lane with the oncoming traffic, we could see the house on its springy flatbed bouncing and hulking like an overanxious bull.

This was not one of those sad double-wides with their vivisected halves roaring by you on the freeway and their backsides marked "wide load." Often when I pass these trailer houses, their cross-sectioned walls battened down by a Visqueen vapor barrier, I stretch to look inside, hoping to see an entire mobile-home life going on: a man in a dingy wife-beater sprawled on a couch watching a grainy TV; a woman making cupcakes in the small island kitchen; a collection of Holly Hobby collector's plates rattling in their wire hangers on the thin dining room wall. But all I see is a hollow cavern of wind-blown emptiness.

Not so this house on the road. Here was a sturdy two-story, complete with a wraparound three-season porch and an attic full of spooky gables. A house worth being torn off its hundred-year-old foundation and rolling with logs and pulleys onto a monstrous flatbed. And on that day, it was making its thirty-mile journey north to the town of Dawson, where it would become, I learned later, a lodge house for weekend hunters. But for now, it was solemn and dignified, moving at a queenly pace, as if rolling through a parade in its honor.

In the distance, we could see the flatbed was flanked on all sides by the flashing red lights of police escorts and the nervous moving crew. Also shadowing the house, moving as it moved, were several orange power company bucket trucks hoisting men in hard hats into the air. The men in the baskets were wearing rubber gloves and held long, slatted poles in their hands. As the house moved, the trucks moved, the men stretching the electrical wires over the matrix of eaves and chimneys with the poles. This was delicate work, dangerous. A small slip and more than one person could have died right before our eyes that morning.

I looked at my watch. It was now 9:20. My husband didn't say anything, just got out of the car and approached one of the road workers. I watched them talk for a while on the side of the road as only men can talk. The county worker spit a prodigious wad onto the blacktop. My husband lifted his shoulders and sank his hands deep into his pockets.

My husband didn't look as if he belonged in this part of the country. He has a thick head of dark wavy hair and soft coffee-brown eyes. He has deep, slanted cheekbones and an arching Roman nose. Even in the more populated and slightly more diverse eastern part of the state where his family lives, people would approach him in stores and say, "You're not from around here, are you?"

If I had gotten out of the car and approached the county worker, the man would have said, "Oh, you're one of the Marquart girls." So identifiable to the region are my family features—a narrowness of chin and angularity of eyes—that I'm sometimes called Little Felix by perfect strangers. But this is how small my hometown is. Even when my husband approached him, the county worker still said, "Oh, you're on your way to Felix's funeral." How did he know this? Why else would someone wearing dress slacks who looks like he's not from around here be on this road at this time of day, unless he were going to a funeral. I looked at my watch. It was 9:25.

My husband turned in the wind and walked back to the van. I could tell by the look on his face the news was not good. "Twenty minutes," he said, getting in and slamming the car door. "They've got to move the house before we can pass."

I looked around at the standing water in the ditches. There was almost enough dry room to pull the van off the blacktop, down the grassy incline, and make a quick getaway into town, but with all the cops around, I was not about to transform into Cousin Daisy from *The Dukes of Hazzard* and invite the pursuit of the drunken sheriff. This was how catastrophes happened, I knew from experience—one bad decision followed another.

Had I done this on purpose? Gotten up a little later than I should have at the hotel, taken a little too long to get dressed before we checked out, so that I could arrive here at this moment. Three miles down the road my father was laid out in the Nickisch Funeral Parlor, the spooky building we'd race by when we were kids, on our way from school, past the grain elevators and across the tracks to get to downtown.

There was a death game we used to play: First, you'd cup your palm against someone else's palm. Then you'd run your thumb up and down the back of your own hand, while at the same time running your fingers along the back of the other person's hand. Then you'd scream and pull your hand away. It was eerie. You could feel the backside of your own hand with your thumb, but the other side, the part that was someone else's hand, was numb against the stroke of your fingers.

"This is what death feels like," we'd whisper to each other in a creepy voice. It was as if the other half of your hand was nothing more than a numb shape in this world. It was busy, we theorized, doing advance work in the other world, being a hand for you across that unknown threshold to which your now half-a-feeling hand would eventually be pulled.

I thought of my father's body dressed in a blue suit, lying parallel to the horizon inside a steel blue coffin lined with satin. I didn't want to see his hands held together in eternal prayer, a black rosary wound around his fingers. I didn't want to shake the thin, sympathetic hand of the undertaker or admire the sheaf of wheat bound with a blue ribbon and placed inside his coffin. I didn't want to overhear family friends marvel at *how good he looks,* and I did not want my mother to force me to get up close and stroke his lapel one last time before they closed the lid for good.

I wanted to remember those hands shuffling a deck of cards, dealing ten to me, ten to him, picking up spares and slapping down discards as he looked to complete his run of queens or diamonds or hearts. And when I snapped my fan of cards down on the table and gave him my rummy smile, I wanted him to rise again and scream in playfulness, "You had my gin card!" and chase me around the house with a shoe until my mother made us stop.

I wanted to remember him scruffing the top of my head, messing my hair, boxing my ears, and saying, "Ah, you're just a rotten kid."

"Wah," I wanted to protest back, "I am not."

I wanted to picture him anywhere but the Nickisch Funeral Parlor—on the couch at home with the remote in his hand, or in the hospital after his last heart attack with the plunger in his hand calling for more medication.

One spring morning when I was about thirteen, my mother asked me to drive the pickup to the north field to take my father his lunch. He had been seeding the land for weeks, and this quarter section was the last to be done. The water levels were high that year, and this particular field had a slope and a small spring in the center. Even under normal conditions, it never dried to more than a slough halfway through the summer.

My father adored straight, even rows, and he loathed wasted acreage. Each year, he circled the wet spot, seeding as close in as possible. How many times as a child had I seen him walking home after he had gotten the tractor stuck near that spring? From the second story of our farmhouse, I could observe him a mile away, walking along the section line, his short legs jutting sharply in front of him as he stamped toward the yard to get another tractor to pull the first tractor out.

When he'd get closer, you could see he'd be swinging his seed cap by his side. And with his hat off, you could make out the leathery sunburned darkness of his face, smudged and dirty from planting, set against the pallor of his bone-white forehead—the one place that lived a pristine, sunless life under the constant protection of his seed cap. And when he'd get close enough to be addressed, my mother would dare to ask, "What happened?" and he'd storm by and shout, "Goddamit."

That day when I drove out to my father in the north field, I sat on the gravel road in the pickup with the cooler beside me on the seat. I watched my dad go around in circles seeding the circumference of the springy spot. It was common to have to wait like this. Farming was serious business, and you were just a kid. You could afford to wait and listen to the radio until the next row was finished.

He circled and circled with the tractor, then got too close to the spring, cut too deep with one of the big back tires, its deep grooves spinning in place, clogged and slick with dark mud. He was trying to back his way out of the mess when he jackknifed the seeder attached to the tractor, and his other back wheel slid down the incline into the mud.

The angry groan of the tractor's engine roared against the quiet backdrop of the morning. The grinding gears gnashed as he rocked the tractor back and forth. The wheels dug down in search of pay dirt, anything solid for the deep rubber grooves to catch on, but the tires only spun around smooth and mud-caked.

And just when he was about to give up, just about to cut the engine, pull the brake, and hop down off the tractor, I saw the front end begin to elevate.

First, the front tires lifted off the ground, then the front end rose higher and higher, carrying my father into the air. It happened so slowly there was time to contemplate the outcome. Would the balance shift and the tractor flip backward over him? This is the most common story of the plains: the blood sacrifice. Each year some farmer must die on his machinery.

My father grasped the steering wheel and slowly stood up, leaning his small body forward to counteract the light front end. I watched all this from the pickup, unable to move or help. It was a moment of sheer weights and balances—the physical world ticking off its equations, none of which included me.

I turned off the radio and waited with my fingers on the door handle. And that is when my father looked in my direction, to see if I was registering all this. Our eyes met, and I could see that he wasn't frightened at all, that he was just his usual self—small and fierce and impatient to know what would happen next.

That's the way I want to imagine him that last day in the hospital. Except for the beeping equipment and the health workers trying to save his life, he was alone. But I want to be there floating above him. And when that part of him that is now gone begins to lift up, I want to meet his eyes, so that I am the last thing he sees. So that he will remember me—the daughter who watches silently by the side of the road, the one who is getting this all down.

At 9:30 on the morning of my father's funeral, I told my husband to turn our van around, to abandon our spot in the column of cars accumulating on the shoulder waiting for the house on the road to pass. The starter zinged to action, and he pulled onto the lane, making a textbook three-point turn on the highway.

My strategy was to circumnavigate the house on the road by driving the section lines. As a kid I had driven the pickup along these back roads, taking lunch out to the men in the fields. As a teenager, I had brought carloads of friends out here to find a safe place to drink and party. As a young woman, I had directed men out here to park. For over twenty years since leaving home, I have driven past this land on Highway 3, never once bothering to wander from the safety of the paved road. But surely, I thought, even after all these years, I could navigate the back roads of my own family land.

A few hundred feet ahead of us was the turnoff to a section line I remembered driving as a child. It was marked by two fifteen-foot pillars of rocks in the corner of the field.

"There." I pointed. "Turn in there."

Every North American generation of my family has contributed layers to those rock piles. The largest stones forming the base were hauled with oxen from the fields by my great-grandparents in the initial land clearing. The ones in the middle were moved with horses by my grandparents. The ones near the top were gathered by tractor and placed there by my immediate family each year as we picked rocks.

From inside the air-conditioned van, I studied the pillars as we turned onto the section line. My palms began to sweat. A heat rose in my body. In one rush, I remembered what it had taken out of our youthful skins to gather and collect those stones.

In the bright morning light, the piles gleamed like shrines. Slowly, I began to discern the shapes of three red foxes reclining among the rocks. They were blending into the cracks, sunning themselves on the warm stones. They followed our slow movement with a wary gaze, licking their silky gold coats with their long snouts. We stared back in silence as we turned off the highway.

The morning took on a strange feel. The first thing we noticed was that the dirt roads we were driving quickly lost their shoulders; then the two grassy tire tracks dwindled down to one lane. Now we are on our way, I thought, going deeper into the middle of nowhere.

As each road disappeared, I instructed my husband to turn onto another lane and then another. Each dwindled into a grassy path. How could this be? What had become of the solid grid of section lines? I looked around and realized how much the shape of the land had changed in the twenty-five years since I had driven these back roads.

The strict squares of my father's wheat and flax crops had turned into roving fenceless fields of grass. Then I remembered my mother commenting during a long-ago phone conversation that the first thing my brother did when he took over the farm was get rid of all the domestic animals and tear down all the fences.

My brother explained later that he had turned some of the land over to the Conservation Reserve Program, the CRP, which gives farmers financial incentives to take their land out of production and seed it back to grass. It was a good program for my brother, who, in early spring, could calculate the cost to seed, fertilize, and harvest a crop for one season and know (not even factoring in the cost of his own labor) that the current wheat prices would not allow him to break even.

So the CRP is good for the farmers, good for the wetlands and the waterfowl. It's good for the land itself, leaving acres fallow so they can recover from years of production, and it's good for the root system, inhibiting erosion by preventing the spill-off of top soil.

With the annual crops had gone the need to drive heavy equipment through the sections on a regular basis, and so the roads had begun to disappear. We came to a halt finally on a section line that had looked promising, but then we saw that in the distance the road dipped into a large pool of standing water. On the other side of the incline, we could see the track of the road leading out of the puddle and proceeding over another rise.

"I think I can make it," my husband said, revving the engine to get a running start.

"No," I screamed as he began to downshift. I could imagine us walking the three miles through the fields in our formal black clothes—me in my black spiked heels. We had reached a dead end, it was clear. We sat there and appreciated our stuckness. The land spread around us for miles, a silent watching presence.

In parts of North Dakota, when the sun touches just right off the fields of wheat, oats, and flax, the view most resembles an ocean. The young men of my state who ride high over the rolling gold fields, harvesting wheat on long, hot August days admit to hallucinating, not waves of wheat, but great rippling bodies of water.

The pioneers, especially those who had recently made an ocean crossing, saw the sea in the level plains and mixed grass prairies they encountered when they first arrived. "I believe this was once the bottom of a great inland sea," one pioneer woman observed in her journal as she crossed Kansas Territory.

Her observation was correct. Somewhere around 100 million years ago, much of the interior of what is now the United States, including North Dakota, was submerged under a shallow ocean extending in fragments from the Gulf of Mexico to the Arctic Ocean. In the North Dakota Geological Survey office, it is possible to see on display fossil remnants of oceanic creatures that have been recovered from fields.

This great Cretaceous Sea, as geologists have called it, divided the continent into eastern and western shores and deposited several strata of shale and a condensed layering of mud and clay that even today, when the layers are penetrated through digging, reveal the fossils and remains of oysters, fish, crocodiles, sharks, and extinct animals such as diving birds and swimming reptiles that inhabited only sea-water areas.

North Dakota's first state geologist, A. G. Leonard, wrote that about 65 million years ago "the sea withdrew from North Dakota never to return."

Within the last two or three million years, during the Pleistocene Epoch, the topography of the Midwest was trans-formed again by what geologists call the great ice plow-up—the movement of glaciers that smoothed and flattened the land to its present state of undulating hills and ridges and deep sinuses of level earth. The most recent glaciation, the Wisconsinan, began approximately 70,000 years ago and ended 10,000 years ago, carrying and spreading rocks from as far away as the Hudson Bay.

It's difficult to imagine the power of glaciers—a heavy wall of ice, hundreds of feet high, that pushes massive boulders thousands of miles, grinding them to fine powder. Geologists explain that as the glacier moves, the weight of the ice forces the materials on the bottom to creep forward toward the margins of the glacier, spreading deeper and wider across the landmass, dropping debris as it goes.

Under the crushing weight of this ice, the earth is flat-tened and smoothed, and the boulders that move and clash are eventually ground down to the size of small stones and pebbles. Massive rocks are reduced to dirt so fine that it sifts like flour through one's fingers. The glacial drift that was left behind is a heterogeneous mixture of limestone, clay, shale, gravel, and pulverized boulders of quartzite, granite, and hornblende.

The drift that remains makes up the flat, farmable plain of central North Dakota that, by some estimates, goes to depths of hundreds of feet in parts of the state. Part of this till is the topsoil that fed me in my youth and has sustained my family now for four generations.

I knew these gravel roads and fields first as a flaming impatient youth, a restless teenager scanning the horizon for all possible methods of escape. For the next twenty-five years, I knew them through the airtight windows of cars, arming myself like an astronaut entering a rarefied environment, only returning home for the most necessary or solemn occasions.

On the morning of my father's funeral, as we were stranded on the section line, I looked around and tried to imagine what it would be like to live out your whole life, as my parents and grandparents had, in one place—to walk and drive its length every day of every season, to be loath to leave it. To know all its turnings in every kind of weather, the colors that its slopes take on, to know its plants and trees, its smells and tendencies, where it drains and thrives and where it gathers water and fails to produce. My father loved this gentle bowl of land with a devotion and intensity usually reserved for wives and children.

Between the land in Bryant Township where my father was born and raised and the land northeast in Streeter Township where my mother was born and raised, everything of significance that has happened to my family on this continent in the last hundred years has happened on that twenty-five mile by twenty-five mile grid of land.

On the day of my father's funeral, I looked around at the acres of windblown grass. I breathed deep and said to my father, who was a trickster in life, "Okay, what are you trying to show me?"

I looked to the right and noticed for the first time an abandoned farmstead. The buildings were broken down to partial frames and toppling foundations. From what remained I could see it had been a two-room shack with a small barn and a chicken coop set deep back in the lot. Somewhere behind the small stand of trees, there was likely to be a small grouping of shallow, unmarked graves—someone's stillborn child or a great-grandmother buried in a spot no one knows to visit.

The tripod of the windmill rose into the sky. Only a few of the weathered tines hung on, long ago abandoning all hope of catching the necessary wind to bring water up from a well. From the architecture of the ruin, it was possible to date the period of abandonment as the early 1900s.

Here was someone's forty acres and a mule, a hopeful beginning followed by an anonymous, tragic ending. The Midwest is full of them. Take any back road off a paved highway and you'll see this scene repeated again and again. The people who once lived here are known forever to no one, and they belong nowhere—the land spread around us too capable of returning all stories to silence.

While we who survive on this land fear losing ourselves to it, those of us who run away are never free of it. That morning, I thought about what geologists say: It's likely that we're in the middle of an interglacial, and that the ice will come again, crush through, brush, and plane down this land to new, unrecognizable shapes.

In geological time, thousands to millions of years, I realize this is nothing I need to worry about. But I think about the generations of my family who have dedicated their lives to keeping our name tied to this parcel of land for 110 years, using all their strength, resources, energy, and imagination to outwit the forces, natural or otherwise, that would so easily strip us of this sense of belonging. And I think about how I have benefited from the sense of rootedness that this place has afforded me as I have cast about, rootless in the world.

That morning we left the abandoned farmstead behind. We put the van in reverse and backed out of the dead end road. We made our way back to the highway through the maze of fading and disappearing paths. At the intersection with the rock piles, we saw the three smiling foxes. They turned their heads and watched us idle by again, going in the other direction.

We arrived at the intersection of Highway 3 just in time to see the house on the road pass by in solemn procession with its entourage of bucket trucks and moving-company pickups. I looked at the clock in the dashboard. It was only 9:40. Amazing. We would make it in time for the funeral. After the house on the road was safely past, we pulled onto Highway 3, rolled up the windows, turned on the AC, and cruised into town.

Several times, in the years since that morning, I have returned to that section line and turned by the pillars of rock. The stones are still there, but never the smiling foxes. I have passed up and down those roads looking for the disappearing set of pathways and for the abandoned farmstead my husband and I encountered that morning.

A few times, I've asked my brother to drive that countryside with me. It's his land now; he knows every inch of it. He slips his rifle in the gun rack just in case we see something interesting to shoot at, and we hop into his pickup.

We have driven up and down those back roads, trying to locate the abandoned farm I saw on the day of my father's funeral—the broken windmill, the remnants of a foundation of a two-room house, the stand of trees, and the falling fences. Although my brother says he believes me each time I describe the place, he and I have never been able to find it.

2

THE LAND HUSBAND

I owe my existence to rain, to the strong uncaring rain that my mother walked home in from her waitressing job one evening in 1948, from which my father rescued her by offering her a ride. Conception through the agency of water comes as a blessing in a place that yields only sixteen inches of precipitation a year. More likely to be born to the endless dust or the incessant wind.

Did he see her first as a woman rushing down the sidewalk with her collar pulled up around her neck? Did she turn at the small honk of a horn as the car pulled up to the curb?

How much in life depends upon a sunny forecast with a rainy outcome, a forgotten umbrella? One turn down an anonymous street reveals a woman walking in the rain. An unknown street becomes *the* street. One offer turns into a lifetime of offers. My mother doesn't remember the make or model of the car, but she remembers the offer from this man, my father, seven years her senior, but still young and good-looking.

Years before he met my mother, my father danced his way through World War Two. Scarred lungs from a childhood bout with pneumonia made him unsuitable for military service. He had done his part stateside, filling up the dance cards of all the local girls whose beaus had flown off to the South Pacific and the European theater. By 1948, when my parents met, he was managing a bar on Main Street, which is how he spotted her, the new girl from a neighboring town, working in the local café.

My father was small-boned with dark hair and blue eyes. Pictures of the time reveal he was as handsome as Cary Grant, but he was shorter, lean and graceful like Fred Astaire. My mother says that when they first started dating, she had difficulty getting a dance with him when they went out. So many women had prior claims to him as a dance partner. The war was over, the beaus had come home and were now husbands, but they were no more graceful than when they'd gone off to fight.

The problem was the polka; my mother could not master it. She tried to learn the dance, but there was a missing step she could not identify (and my father would not be bothered to show her) that kept her from gliding as smoothly as all the other women when they danced with my father.

Every weekend my mother sat forlornly on the benches surrounding the dance floor, a stranger in this new town, watching her date, my father, whirl by again and again in the laughing arms of more light-footed women. Finally another man from town took pity on her, lifted her to her feet and showed her the hidden step, the half hop in mid-step, that would create the appearance of floating. If not for this kind man, it's possible that none of us children would have been born.

My father was an elderly bachelor of twenty-seven at the time; my mother was twenty. Despite my father's dancing prowess, his graceful frame belied a history of delicate health. The case of pneumonia at three years old had filled his lungs with fluid causing the doctor to pronounce his case hopeless and abandon his treatment. My father had lingered near death.

As a last resort, one of the uncles had summoned the *brauchere*, a midwife and healer in our town who used chants, herbs, and poultices to cure the sick. My father was too young to remember the details, but he often told the story to us, as it had been told to him—how the old woman sat by his bed through the day and night, mumbling prayers over him in German. How she had spoken directly to the illness, warning it to leave his body and burn elsewhere. How she had wrestled with the fever through the long night, insulting it by calling it "little fire," as she fed him internally and doused him externally with a milky remedy made of boiled wormwood, a stinky green weed that for the duration of his life my father refused to spray or cut down when it grew in his fields.

Later he would confess to my mother that he had avoided getting married in his early twenties because he didn't believe he would live to old age. And the situation soon proved grave: by his mid-twenties, the scarring on his lungs from the pneumonia grew into tumors that necessitated the most damaged lung be removed.

This was around the time my mother started dating him. The surgery was so perilous that it had to be done at the Mayo Clinic. Fortunately for him, my mother was a strong young woman, and they were in love. They resolved to get married, if he survived the operation.

On the strength of this agreement, my father headed off to Rochester, Minnesota, in his Uncle John's car with a wad of borrowed cash in his pocket and a promise to my mother that he would call her at such-and-such a time, if he survived the operation.

On the day of the surgery, my mother waited at the allotted time and place for the all-important phone call, which did not come and did not come. Then she went home, had a good long cry, and prepared to begin talking about my father in the past tense—the man I almost married, the man with whom I'd hoped to have children.

Weren't we kids all glad that he did call her hours later when the anesthesia wore off, before our decisive mother wrote him off entirely and set her cap for some other man, landing us all on the planet with different noses, cheekbones, hair, and eye colors? This was how distantly mythic our parents' courtship had seemed to us growing up.

But by the time of my birth, my family was a well-oiled machine. Within four years of marriage, my parents had produced as many children—1950, 1951, 1952, and 1953. They turned us out like Chevys. I appeared in 1956, after a three-year hiatus. Was there a labor dispute between them, a breakdown in union talks, or had my clear-eyed mother simply made adjustments to her new Catholicism? Whatever the reason, my arrival meant we'd be trading in the sedan for a station wagon.

As the last model to come down the assembly line, I ended my parents' procreative efforts. For as Father liked to say when he became overwhelmed with us, once he and Mother determined what was causing children, they promptly put an end to it.

My mother was a Lutheran when she met my father, a scandal where I come from. She converted to Catholicism when they married, a mixed marriage where I come from. Even though she'd been through all the necessary rites and sacraments by the time I was born, I like to think it was me, her fifth child, who transubstantiated her into a true Catholic.

What self-respecting Catholic woman stops at four children? I can recall several Catholic families in my hometown with over twenty living children, not to mention the gaps in the birth order that indicate the two or three stillbirths or young children lost to illness or accident. The Catholic mother in a family like this would have to start early and produce, on average, one child every sixteen months for the duration of her childbearing years.

In my hometown, Catholic families are large enough to be basketball teams, baseball teams, football teams—both sides, offense and defense. They're a rural version of the Kennedys, happy and self-sufficient, whole Sundays of fun rolling around together on endless green farm lawns.

But our parents, it seemed to us growing up on the farm, were hopeless dullards. We had no vacations, no road trips to monumental sights. We went to Bismarck two times a year to shop, and only on days when the weather was too miserable to work. In addition to the wheat, we grew flax, oats, barley, and alfalfa. We had chickens and eggs, sold cream, and raised livestock for slaughter. We had a vegetable garden larger than the hobby farm acreages of most of my adult friends, and we were dairy farmers, milking up to seventy-five Holsteins at one time.

Dairy farming is as close as one can come to slavery and still be a technically free person. You must be on site every morning and evening to milk cows. In addition to the farm, my mother worked part time at a clothing store in Napoleon, and my father was now part owner, with his brother Ben, of a bar in town called The Spot. Both he and Mother worked at The Spot some mornings and afternoons, and always on Friday and Saturday nights.

As children we knew our parents largely in the context of work. We went to church early on Sundays, then we spent the rest of the morning cleaning the bar from the mess of Saturday night. I still remember the incense-and-candle smell of church being replaced by the ash-and-yeast odor of stale cigarette butts and spilled beer when Dad swung open the front door of the bar and we piled in to clean. If we worked fast, we each got a Walnut Crush as a reward.

On a farm where survival hangs in the balance, there is no tolerance for tantrums. We children were expected to be well behaved and hardworking. No room to be moody, temperamental, or high-strung. Yet all manner of extravagance was foisted on our Holsteins. We knew them as individual personalities with names like Moony or Queenie or White Socks, usually based on the black-and-white markings on their coats.

Our Holsteins were idiosyncratic and particular, too sensitive to be milked by strangers or even distant blood relations. They had specific likes and dislikes, ways they could and could not be touched. Each cow preferred a certain stanchion, for example, and you had to know when to let her into the barn to be milked, so you didn't let in another cow at the same time who liked the very same stanchion. It would be mayhem.

They were like aristocracy, these Holsteins, expecting a specific quantity and quality of oats waiting for them when they slipped their heads through the stanchions. Their level of happiness determined how much milk we extracted from their teats at five in the morning and five in the afternoon, the two times a day we milked them. This is why dairy farmers can never travel to any destination from which they cannot return by five o'clock the same day.

The word *husband* in its earliest origins means to be bound to the house, or house-bound—a peasant, for example, who owns his own house and land. It also describes one who manages his affairs with skill and thrift, as in, to husband one's resources. In its most literal sense, the husbandman is one who tills and cultivates the soil.

As the word implies, a husbandman marries himself to the land, agreeing to nurture and care for it over a lifetime. In the history of my family, for as far back as it is possible to know, we have been husbands of the land, or farmers, a word that takes its origins from *firma,* or earth. On the North American continent, my great-grandfather reinitiated the contract when he immigrated to Dakota Territory in 1885 and took up a land claim.

My ancestors believed that rain follows the plow—that the practice of farming a place, even an arid place, would transform its meteorology—and their experience had given them nothing to prove otherwise. Two hundred years ago, in 1803, my great-great-great-grandparents had immigrated to Russia from Alsace-Lorraine along the Rhine River in Western Europe. They were royalists on the run from the French Revolution. Answering an offer of free land from Czar Alexander I, they migrated east and took up virgin land claims near the Black Sea, breaking sod on the Russian steppe, an ancient grassland that had run like a corridor across Eastern Europe, Siberia, and Mongolia for centuries.

So when my great-grandfather Marquart fled Russia and arrived in Dakota Territory in 1885, he encountered something entirely familiar—another treeless steppe, the ancient grassland of the North American Great Plains that had been home for thousands of years to native tribes such as the Arikara, Hidatsa, Mandan, Missouri, Lakota, Dakota, and Yankton Sioux people.

Richard Manning noted in his book, *Grassland,* that "the settlers came to the plains flush with this notion . . . that the wilderness is in need of taming and the desert is in need of being made to bloom." In one ungrazed stretch of grassland,

Manning wrote, one could identify 250 species of plants inhabiting a single site. "With work, a plow, and chemicals, a wheat farm drags the count down to one species."

First-person accounts taken from those who broke sod describe it as a violent popping sound, like a zipper opening or pistons firing. Beneath this complex tangle of roots they found a topsoil—rich and deep in some places, sandy and rock-filled in others. For better or worse, once the land was cleared, they set to work cultivating and shaping it in order to make a life from it.

As a daughter of agriculture, I understood early that the relationship with family land was painful, satisfying, devastating. It was all-consuming, the most passionate kind of love affair.

In *Grassland,* Richard Manning documented that this ancient and complex root system that dominated the central plains most often defeated the farmers who tried to find sustenance from it. "Their ancestors filled poorhouses, insane asylums, and graveyards in a battle against the grass."

And this story was repeated in counties all over the Great Plains. Wes Jackson reported in *Becoming Native to This Place,* that his neighbor, Nick Fent, the owner of 240 acres in Nebraska, has researched and written a seventy-year history of his three contiguous eighty-acre plots of land in Rice County.

Fent chronicled the negative spiral of land ownership on and beyond the hundredth meridian—the cycles of "drought when crops failed completely; wet years, when the creek bottom corn fields were too soft to work; and plagues of grasshoppers that ate everything from cornstalks to hoe handles." Among the plagues that followed were blight, extreme poverty, isolation, alcoholism, and insanity.

As Fent researched the succession of deeds to his land, he discovered that between 1885 and 1955, fourteen families had tried and failed to survive on what was now his center eighty acres—"Dell, Hawkins, Decious, Crowel, Minor, Carnal, Curtis, Loughridge, Scholl, Haley, Ashman, Wetchel, Walker, and Mills."

Reading this list of surnames is sobering. My great-grandfather's gift to us, his progeny, is that he managed to keep four generations of our family on the land, out of the record books, numbered among the survivors rather than the failures at subsistence farming. I begin to feel the miracle of it. At the same time, I understand too well the costs.

The first vehicle I ever drove was my father's tractor in the hayfield. How good a driver can you be at ten, your legs too short to reach the pedals, your head barely clearing the steering wheel?

In the field hauling bales, I negotiated the bumpy rows with the tractor and its large flatbed trailer. I was the youngest girl—big teeth and spindly arms and legs—no good for lifting, so I had to be the driver. I'd climb up the gigantic tires of the Allis-Chalmers and plant myself behind the wheel. To engage the pedals, I'd have to shift the entire length of my body to the right or left, hang onto the wheel, and extend my foot as far as possible.

Walking behind the tractor in the field are my sisters and my brother, only a few years older than I, heaving and hoeing alfalfa bales onto the flatbed. If I buck the tractor by accident or lurch the clutch or accelerate too quickly, I will look back and find them all glaring, red-faced and angry at me.

In front of the tractor, standing in long vapor streams of heat is my father. He waves his hands to signal me forward as if he's trying to park a 747. He screams two words at me—"Whoa" and "Go"—which look amazingly alike when you're reading lips over the roaring horsepower of a tractor.

Sometimes I go when I'm supposed to whoa. Sometimes I whoa when I'm supposed to go. Everyone is mad at me. All morning and late into the hot afternoon, my father is alternately shocked and horrified at my stupidity, at my inability to follow simple instructions. At night when I go to bed, I can still feel the vibrations of the tractor's steering wheel pulsing through my forearms and palms.

Many years later when I call my oldest sister Kate to verify these memories, she confirms them, then tells me a story I've never heard. In her version, I'm still the driver, but I'm only five. She's twelve. As the oldest, it's her job to prop me in the seat of the tractor, push in the clutch, and get the thing into first gear.

As the tractor begins to idle along, she gets my hands set on the wheel, so that I will steer it straight down the field in an even row. Once she accomplishes this, she jumps off the moving tractor, careful to keep her body clear of the big tires, and joins the others, who are picking rocks and tossing them in the trailer I'm towing.

When I hear this story, I'm stunned that I have no trace memory of it. I imagine myself at five, small for my age, dwarfed in the giant scoop of the tractor seat, my short legs dangling in the air, the hot disk of the sun above me, the big circle of the wheel that I must grasp, and in front of me, the huge open field, the long day of endless rows waiting to be driven.

When I reached the end of each row, my sister's job was to make a run at the tractor and land safely on the moving platform. Then she would turn the tractor around and set me up for steering another row. How she managed all this at twelve, I have no idea.

When I was born, my sister Kate was so excited that she broke into hives. She went to school to tell her second-grade class that she had a new sister, and when her teacher casually asked what my name was, my sister began to weep; she felt so ashamed that she had forgotten my name.

I was her baby-doll girl growing up; our mother was busy with a million other chores, so Kate often was in charge of dressing and bathing me. When I was nine months old, Kate fell down the stairs with me in her arms. When we landed at the bottom, I had a bloody nose, and she had a cut on her chin, but my mother always remembers that my sister cried longer than I did, just from fear of having possibly harmed me.

"It's a wonder we all survived to adulthood," Kate marveled that night we talked on the phone. At that distance, we could laugh about it in disbelief. We were the fortunate ones, averting major catastrophe. But I wonder now what kind of small traumas my oldest sister may have sustained as she planted me behind that wheel, then jumped on and off a moving tractor all day—not only for her safety, but for mine, and for the crush of responsibility that she would have felt if something had happened to me.

My friends who grew up in the other 1960s America, the one with swimming pools and green suburban lawns, find these stories impossible to believe. They say I must be misremembering, adding hardship over time, like those old people who insist they walked ten miles to country school each day, in knee-deep snow, uphill, both ways.

I call my second oldest sister Elizabeth to confirm the stories. She says, yes, she remembers all this. Then she tells me about another time, when we all hauled alfalfa bales in one-hundred-degree heat on the Fourth of July. She remembers this day most acutely because the field bordered Highway 3. She and Kate were teenagers at the time, and they watched the road mournfully as cars full of their best friends and their boyfriends passed by and honked their horns, heading north to the lake.

Despite the peaceful, idyllic look of a farm, it's an easy place to lose one's life. Anyone who has stood beside even the smallest farm implement knows how deadly the machinery can be. Grown men have been crushed under the deep grooves of tractor tires. No year passed in North Dakota without news of someone losing a hand, an arm, an eye, or his life in a farm accident.

People who work around farm machinery every day forget how dangerous it is. A switch gets flipped, and a man is snuffed to death inside his silo, drowning in a sea of the grain he's just harvested. Farmers with forty years' experience get absentminded and reach into a stalled baler or the turbine of a combine and are dead within minutes.

As young children, we had no business being near farm equipment, much less operating it. All my life, I've wondered why every industry in the country has laws to protect children—garment, meat-packing, mining, shipping—but the children of agriculture are left to work, according to their parents' needs and discretion, on family farms.

Was it spring or fall, that Saturday afternoon when the phone call came with the news about Benny Maas. We were flying kites in our big backyard. I remember most the crispness of the wind and the way my mother's voice calling from the house rose above the flapping of the kites.

It would not be the last funeral I attended for a boy from school who was killed in the fields. I was ten. Do I remember it so vividly because before the news came, the day had been so perfect—flying kites, the thrill of feeling the tug of this fragile contraption bobbing in the wind?

Benny was fifteen, my brother's age. Like my brother, he was an only son. His sister was in my class. She was a shy blond girl who rarely spoke. But now I wonder if her chronic silence, her constantly averted eyes, preceded or followed her brother's death. For a long time after that, it was not possible to look at her without thinking that her brother was dead, and that it could have been me. I could have been the girl in class with the dead brother.

In my family, we all understood from the beginning that my brother's life was claimed for the farm. From the time he was a young boy, he worked as an equal beside my parents, as early and late in the day as they did. He rose at five o'clock with them each morning to milk the cows no matter what the weather. When he became a teenager, he worked longer, harder hours than anyone, in the fields at harvest time, the tractor going up and down the rows at night. Only the dim headlights of the tractor could be seen from a distance in the darkness.

I remember his soft blue eyes peering out from a face caked black with dirt when he'd get home at eleven at night during harvest time. My mother would have held a plate of food for him, and he'd sit hunched at the dark kitchen table eating alone, his arms, his neck, his jeans, his boots caked with dirt from the fields. The next morning, he was expected to be up early for milking then out in the fields for another eighteen-hour day.

From my earliest memory of my brother, he was quiet and gentle. While my father was explosive, growing more impatient and frustrated with anything that did not cooperate with him, my brother took after my mother's father, Grandpa Geist. They were calm tinkerers. They could fix anything. Animals and machines purred in their hands.

Even though Nick was only a few years older than I, he was paternal with me as a child. When I was five, I got sick and had to take a vile-tasting medicine. After a few nights of watching me cry and thrash as my mother forced the thick pink syrup down my throat, my brother gathered every stuffed animal in the house on my bed, then cooed and coddled me until I allowed him to spoon the medicine into my mouth.

After what happened to Benny Maas, my feelings grew more tender toward my brother. I gave him extra potatoes when I dished up his food; I plumped up his pillows and tucked in his bed sheets with greater care. I worried about the tired groans I heard from his room early in the morning when my father called him from the bottom of the steps for chores.

I hated to think about him going out in the cold; I wanted to spare him, but I didn't have the strength or the will to offer myself in his place. I came to understand that he worked so hard because there was only one of him, a boy, and there were so many of us girls.

On the farm, my mother worked as hard as any man. My sisters and I worked according to our own abilities. But my brother did the most perilous work with my father—going out in blizzards, staying up all night during calving season, running the combine during the harvest—just as Benny Maas had. People said the farm accident that killed Benny had been some slip with the equipment. I never knew the details. Some said his father was possibly at fault. I have always wondered, how does a family recover from this?

My mother was nineteen years old that rainy night she accepted a ride from my father. From pictures, I can reconstruct her beauty—her wide open smile, her good posture, her straight white teeth. Once she got into the car, there was no hope for her. She told me all this one Christmas Eve, a few years after my father's death. It was just the two of us, and we talked late into the night.

As soon as my parents met, they became wildly prolific. Each year brought another child. My mother was so fertile, my father joked, that all he had to do was set his pants on the bed and she would be pregnant again.

In this way, Catholic families are a pyramid scheme. In a family of thirteen-plus children like those in my hometown, the oldest ones raise the middle ones, and the youngest children know their oldest siblings almost as distant uncles and aunts who come home for special occasions.

When the children grow up, if they proliferate at even a fraction of the rate of their parents, the family grows exponentially. For many Catholic families in my hometown, it's impossible to get three generations under one roof. For Christmas or Thanksgiving, they must rent a dance hall or the Veterans of Foreign Wars or the Golden Age Club.

Here agriculture meets Catholicism in a perfect confluence of needs. The church gets more souls; the farm gets more workers. The object of so much trying was the production of boys. Most often, the result was more girls. My own family is a case-in-point: four girls, one boy. And in the centennial books of neighboring towns this pattern is repeated for page after page of formal family photographs—the parents dressed in solemn black, seated front and center, flanked on all sides by beautiful girls, smiling apologetically at the camera, with a few thin boys tucked into their ranks.

Klaus Theweleit noted in *Male Fantasies* that "women's bodies are considered objects and raw material, the terrain of man's own production." I have only to think about two of my great-grandmothers—Barbara Hulm Marquart, who died in childbirth, and Katherine Dockter Hoffer, who died from complications following childbirth—to confirm the truth of Theweleit's claim.

And yet, as a daughter of agriculture, I must recognize that the men of my family sacrificed their bodies as painfully and completely to the land as did the women.

Growing up, I believed I was surrounded by the most austere, pragmatic, hardworking people. But now I know that we were hopeless romantics when it came to land—the worst sort of high-stakes gamblers, betting the farm and all of our lives every day when we went into the fields. Our success was dependent on the weather, the government, the ancient gods of catastrophe, the Chicago Board of Trade, all forces out of our control. Yet we persevered.

We were working together toward one goal, elegant in its simplicity—keeping the land in the family. Even to me, the youngest, the purpose was clear. We were all needed to accomplish the task. Our survival was at stake. There was no room for error or waste.

I respect the virtue of what we struggled for, even more as I get older, and I take pride in our accomplishments. But I also grieve the high personal cost. It's a hard thing to let go of—the sadness of a lost childhood, being saddled with something so heavy so early.

And so it happened that I was in my mother's womb the night in 1956 when my parents had the worst fight of their married lives. I learned this over forty years later, the Christmas Eve I spent alone with my mother and we talked late into the night.

After my parents married, they moved the family away from Napoleon, our small hometown. They imagined a different life for us in the city. They bought a two-story brick house with a concrete stoop and a leafy yard on Avenue A in Bismarck. My father worked at a hardware store as an appliance salesman. My mother was a homemaker. These are their professions, as listed on my birth certificate.

My father often said that he had seventy-five dollars to his name when he married my mother in 1949. Seven years and four children later, they were approaching solvency. Money was accumulating in their savings account. They managed this by renting out the top floor and the basement apartment of the house on Avenue A; the whole family of six people—such as it was before my arrival—lived crowded together on the main floor.

But on that night in 1956 when my mother was pregnant with me, my father came home and announced that they would be moving back home to take over the family farm. He made this decision by some reasoning forever unknown to my mother. She may have seen it coming—the weekly sales meetings he loathed, the hard retail floor he stood on all day, the sales quotas rising higher each week, the migraines he suffered every night.

My father was the seventh child in a family of ten children. Each of his four brothers—three older and one younger—had already tried, in his own time, to take over the family farm from my grandfather. Each had been rebuffed.

I have an early 1950s photo of my grandfather, Joseph Marquart, standing on the back steps of the farmhouse. He's a short man like all the people in my family, but he looks tall because the photo is shot from the ground looking up, from what Charlton Heston calls the Moses angle. In the photo, my grandfather is trim, his posture is straight. He's wearing suspenders with his hands thrust in his pants pockets and his chin in the air. A tabby cat turns at his feet on the stoop.

I imagine the drama that unfolded as my father's brothers, each in his own time, tried to take over the family farm—Ben, the gentle, older brother; Frank, who was a handsome sharp dresser; Jay, who was funny and hardworking; and hot-headed Pete. I see each brother taking a run up the stoop at my grandfather, trying to knock the old goat—with his wiry frame, his lantern jaw, his thick shock of gray hair—off the mountain.

Not one had succeeded; each had spun off onto other farms or into other occupations. Now it was 1956, my grandfather was dying of lung cancer, and no sons remained to take over the farm.

This left my father, with his history of delicate health. Perhaps it's something unspoken in farm families, but it's something understood: Whoever takes over the land has to be able to work hard, beyond exhaustion, and has to be able to produce a line of sons to ensure that the land will not go out of the family.

I understand now that my father never intended to become a farmer. He loved music and singing and dancing. He was sensitive and studious. He prided himself on being the first boy in his family to have finished high school. This is one reason Mother married him—she was so confident that with him she'd never spend another day of her life on a farm.

Sometimes it's a mystery, the stories that get repeated in a family and those that remain unspoken. After my mother told me about the fight they'd had over my father's decision to take over the family farm, it took me three days to formulate the question: "How did you ever resolve the argument?"

My mother turned and looked at me with surprise, as if no one had ever asked her that question before. *How had they resolved it?* She seemed to be thinking, as if wondering it for the first time herself.

Then she shrugged and said, "Oh, I just gave in." And with that simple answer I understood more about my mother than I'd known in an entire lifetime of being her daughter.

I remember her frustration with us when we were children, the slamming cupboard doors, the rushing about, the preoccupation with polished floors. Now I realize she had been in the middle of the hardest job of her life. Every time she looked around, there was another one of us to care for. The work on the farm was endless, the stakes were unbearably high, and none of it had been her decision.

My mother was a worker and an organizer, a hardheaded pragmatist. More than anyone, she would have known what it would take to make my father's dream a reality. And she would have seen it all in one glance—the toll my father's nostalgia was going to take on all of us.

But in a family photograph from my first birthday in 1957, my father stands smiling in front of our farmhouse with his five children. I'm tucked in the crook of his arm, wearing a homemade white cotton dress, looking like everybody's pudding dumpling.

My brother stands on my father's right side, his nose scrunched up, giggling for the camera. The fingers of my father's right hand are spread wide on my brother's shoulder. It's a gentle gesture, not a proprietary one, as if to say he is proud of having this very son. My three older sisters are lined up on my father's left side wearing the identical white cotton dresses my mother has sewn in their three different sizes.

There's no question my mother arranged the photo; her mark of perfection is everywhere, down to my three sisters' neat white anklets and the immaculately ironed dress shirt my father is wearing. Within one year, this remarkable woman has marshaled our resources and shaped us into her own particular order.

My mother is not pictured, because she is the one holding the camera. Only a trace of her exists in the photo, a long shadow that falls across the lower left corner of the picture. Hers is like the hand of God in this way—nowhere visible, everywhere in evidence.

Before words, before sentences, before paragraphs and parts of speech, there was only the sound of my mother's voice. Before the interruption of consonants from the outside world, there was one unbroken string of vowels—the *aeiou* of her womb—and for a long time after that, only the *mum, mum, mum* of my mother's arms, the steady thump of her heartbeat then the *doodla, doodla* of her knee, quieting me in church.

There was the *dominus vobiscum* of Mass, and the thrum of the pipe organ on the pew. Later came the *bing, bong* bass of my father's country western music playing loud on the stereo downstairs before breakfast, and the *deedla, deedla* of the accordion at dances. Then there was the *hochzeit,* the wedding celebration.

I remember circles. The swirling cuff of my father's pant leg, the layered hem of my mother's skirt. A neighbor lady polkas by, the one who yells so loud at her kids every night we can hear her across the still fields. She has a delicious smile on her face tonight and the creamy half moon of her slip shows under her long, tight dress.

The dance hall is an octagon, eight sides squaring off in subtle shades to make a circle. The Ray Schmidt Orchestra is on the bandstand, a family of musicians. The two young daughters wear chiffon dresses, patent leather shoes and white tights as they patter away at the bass and drums. Their mother, her lips a wild smear of red, stomps and claws chords on the dusty upright.

The father and the son take turns playing the accordion, the bellowing wheeze, the squeeze of notes, the *oom-pa-pa.* Years later this son will become minorly famous—wildly famous in this county—when he makes it onto the *Lawrence Welk Show.* He'll be groomed as the new accordion maestro, the heir apparent to Myron Floren, who was the heir apparent to

Lawrence Welk. This is polka country, the deep vinegar core of the sauerkraut triangle. The accordion is our most soulful, ancestral instrument.

Someone is getting married. An uncle? A cousin? Who knows. Everyone is a cousin in this town. I have a new dress with a flared skirt and a matching ribbon. I get to stay up late. This has been going on for hours and promises to go on for hours more. Old ladies in shawls, looking like everyone's grandma, sit around the edges of the dance floor, smiling with sad eyes at the dancers.

A rotund man who looks like everyone's grandpa makes the rounds with a tray of shot glasses, spinning gold pools of homemade whiskey. "Red eye," they call it, wedding schnapps. The recipe is one cup burnt sugar, one cup water, one cup Everclear, 190 proof. The old man bends low with the tray of glasses—one sip for everybody, no matter how small. Sweet burning warmth down my throat, sweet swirling dizziness.

Someone lifts me up. An uncle? A cousin? I have no idea. He dances me around the circle in the air, my short legs dangling beneath me, then returns me to my seat. The old women receive me, straightening my new skirt and ribbons.

The music speeds up. The accordion pumping chords like a steam engine—the waltz, the butterfly, the schottische, the polka. The dance floor flexes like a trampoline. Women swing by in the arms of their partners. They kick their big legs and throw back their bouffants. High whoops and yips emit from their bosoms.

On the dance floor, my father clasps my mother's hand and pulls her tight. The building heaves, the accordion breathes. Faster and faster they spin, my father's arm secured around my mother's waist. If left to itself, gravity could take over, centrifugal force could spin them out, away from each other.

My mother smiles behind her cateye glasses, confident of her partner. All night they reel circles around the room, two young, strong bodies enjoying this thrill of almost spinning out while being held safely in. My parents. Everyone agrees they are the best dancers on the floor.

3

THE MOST FAMOUS PERSON FROM NORTH DAKOTA

When we were kids, our parents subjected us to cruel and unusual punishment: They forced us to watch Lawrence Welk with them. Every Saturday night after supper, our dish towels flew. Supper was what we called the evening meal back then, what my mother still calls it even though most of us have moved away and now call it dinner.

We hated doing dishes. We lingered over our reflections in the stainless steel frying pans. We excused ourselves to the bathroom more times than necessary. Our mother urged us on. She stood at the sink pulling silverware from the scorching water, barking out commands about which Tupperware container went with which leftovers, as we swabbed counters and dried plates.

It was not until every dish was put away, not until the sink was wiped down and the chrome polished to a glisten, that we could retreat to the living room, where my father already waited—all of us ready for the first sight of bubbles floating up from behind the bandstand, the first yippy tones of clarinets.

What we suffered from back then was a lack of options. These were the black-and-white days of the 1960s. We only had two channels. And what was on that other station? *Gunsmoke* or *Mission Impossible*? I have no idea because my father never let us touch the dial once Lawrence Welk came on.

We watched those "words from our sponsors," commercials from companies like Geritol, Sominex, and Aqua Velva, with the same reverence as we watched the show. These were the people, my father reasoned, who were paying good money to put Lawrence Welk on television. The least we could do was hear what they had to say.

This is the old way of watching television, from the time before the mute button, when checking to see what was on the other station involved getting up from the couch. The people from this era don't watch television in quite the same way as those who came later, who grew up with the white noise of countless channels running constantly in the background.

Many years later, after I became a musician myself and started traveling around the country in a run-down bus, I might be in my motel room, exhausted from an all-night drive and scanning the dial for something good to watch, when I'd happen upon the *Lawrence Welk Show* and then I'd be stuck. I would have to watch it all over again. Because thanks to public television and "viewers like you" we now have Lawrence Welk and his musical family in reruns unto infinity.

All those old-fashioned, song-and-dance tunes where the boy gets too fresh and the girl gets huffy and crosses her arms to show how properly miffed she is. All those smiling women, heavily coiffured in that Aqua Net flip that was so popular back then, which we now know was highly flammable and dangerous to the ozone.

Every woman on the show was pretty in that very-nice-girl way. In their dance numbers they swayed to the music in a row of flowing chiffon, while all those fresh-faced men marched in place, swinging their arms in time to some patriotic anthem—all of them wearing matching polyester suits and shoes dyed to bizarre colors never to be found in nature.

And behind it all with a grin as sly as Quasimodo lurks Lawrence Welk, the maestro puppeteer, baton in hand, smiling ingratiatingly at the camera, accent in tow, his odd syllables grazing over difficult words.

Even back then when I was a kid and forced to like it, those too-cute-for-television introductions struck me as amazingly corny. To Lawrence it seemed everyone was "nice" (pronounced *nize*), "very talented," and, of course, "wunnerful."

And even back then, as my parents exclaimed over how smooth this dancer was or how good that singer was, I was not fooled for one minute. I knew that Lawrence Welk was no Benny Goodman, no Count Basie, even though I had not yet heard of these people. He was no Guy Lombardo, no Duke Ellington, certainly no Louis Armstrong. The accordion was a big tip-off. No for-real bandleader played the accordion. Even in my provincial innocence I was fairly certain of that.

But continue to watch we did, because Lawrence Welk had the distinction of being the most famous person from North Dakota. And we watched because my father insisted we were related to Lawrence Welk. "A distant relative," he assured us, "a shirt-tail cousin," but nevertheless still related.

There's a general feeling in small towns that if you look back far enough, you'll find that everyone, except the imported specialists such as the high school principal and the doctor, is distantly related. Around every corner are more people declaring themselves to be your great-uncle, your third cousin, your step-aunty through marriage on your father's side.

But Cousin Lawrence? Even as a child, this struck me as an alarming possibility. Although he spoke with an accent like that of most of the people in my hometown—first- and second-generation descendants of ethnically German immigrants from Russia—I had a sick feeling that no one on television should sound and look like us.

All of this was lost on my parents, who were dazzled by Welk's wealth and fame. "They say he owns a golf course and a resort near San Diego," my mother offered while Lawrence danced the polka with some lucky member of the studio audience.

"Escondido," my father corrected.

"He just drives up to Hollywood to tape the shows," my mother would say in a golf whisper, like one who had read an insider's report.

Hearing him gossiped about made him feel close, like a relative, but I harbored a hard kernel of disbelief. There was no concrete evidence of our relationship to him. My father swore we got Christmas cards from him for a while. *Along with thousands of other people,* I thought. In his early career, everyone agreed, Welk had stayed with our grandparents in this very house when he passed through town. He played for dances in a huge barn that had once stood at the foot of our hill.

My Grandma Marquart was no longer alive, so I couldn't ask her about Cousin Lawrence. Even this mythohistoric barn had been razed, and a new barn had been built higher up the hill. We found traces of the old barn—fragments of wood shingles, horseshoes, and a rusty nail that I stepped on—but not enough to confirm the veracity of our father's claims.

Years later when I checked the family genealogy, I discovered that I was indeed related to Lawrence Welk. My great-grandmother, Barbara Welk Weigel, was a first cousin to Lawrence's father, which makes Lawrence my second cousin, twice removed, if you know how to figure these things out. Close, but not close enough to be included in the will. They had all immigrated to Dakota Territory from Selz, their small village in south Russia in the 1890s. At the very least, we could say we came over on roughly the same boat. But to the people in my hometown, Lawrence Welk was a symbol of something more than just blood and Old World ties. He was the one who got away from North Dakota and had made good.

If you leave Fargo at 9:00 in the morning, going west on I–94, and travel at a reasonable rate of speed, you'll reach south-central North Dakota by noon, just as the sun rises in a hot spike above you. In that time, you'll have passed through the Red River Valley, a lacustrine plain on the eastern border of North Dakota, which is some of the richest farmland in the world and the drainage plain for the Red River, one of the few rivers in the world that flows true north.

Eastern North Dakota is a spacious valley of luminous sky with land so flat, some claim, that you can see the curvature of the earth as you're driving. In geological history, it's the ancient lake bed of the glacial Lake Aggasiz, a body of water that once covered 110,000 square miles, by some estimates, and dipped down from Canada, into Minnesota and the Dakotas. Aside from the Red River, the last vestige of Lake Aggasiz is Lake Winnipeg in Manitoba, itself a substantial lake by today's standards.

Driving west from Fargo on I–94, the freeway that cuts through the state of North Dakota, you'll encounter a road so lonely, treeless, and devoid of rises and curves in places that it will feel like one long-held pedal steel guitar note. If your tires are in proper alignment, you'll only need to tap your steering wheel to keep your car on a straight-ahead path.

Now you are driving deep into the square states. This is the way in which I recently heard a comedian describe the column of states that holds down the center of the country— the Dakotas, Nebraska, Kansas, Oklahoma—a region that spawns both tornadoes and Republicans.

TV news anchors often hail from this part of the world, as do the most innocent female characters in movies and prime-time TV dramas. Being blond, fresh-faced, and midwestern makes their descent into ruthless behavior in places like Los Angeles and New York all the more tragic.

"We are the folks presidents talk to when times require," Sylvia Griffith Wheeler wrote in her poem "Earthlings." Networks make up women to look like us "who will not trade their bleaches, soaps for anything."

This is a region that contains both Garrison Keillor's Lake Wobegon ("where all the women are strong, all the men are good-looking, and all the children are above average") and the Coen Brothers' *Fargo*, the macabre land of murder-by-wood-chipper. Aside from this myth making, the Midwest is a place that's been considered devoid of stories, a flyover region one must endure to get to more interesting places.

Despite its easy inclines and farmable plains, the region was equally unimpressive to its earliest assessors. In the 1820s, Edwin James, the official chronicler of Major Stephen Long's survey, declared the region "a dreary plain, wholly unfit for cultivation," and, of course, "uninhabitable by a people depending upon agriculture for subsistence." It was Edwin James who dubbed the area between the Mississippi and the Rockies the Great American Desert, an indignity from which the region has struggled to recover ever since.

This is the Heartland, the place where Jefferson's idea of a rectangular cadastral survey, the land grid system outlined in the Land Ordinance of 1785, found its most perfect confluence of longitude, latitude, and countryside so well behaved that it laid itself down in neat, even squares for the surveyor's instruments.

Soon enough, as the surveying expedition moved west, the neatness of the grid was foiled by steep valleys, rivers, foothills, and mountains, but here in the monotonous square states, the survey subdivided the land easily into square upon square, each measuring six miles by six miles. What followed, Richard Manning observed in *Grassland,* was a war on roots: "The place was a mess, and it became a young nation's job to fix it with geometry, democracy, seeds, steam, steel, and water."

Such is the situation all of my great-grandparents and grandparents encountered when they arrived between the years of 1885 and 1911. They traveled to the Midwest by train to what was then the end of the line—Eureka, South Dakota. *Eureka*—from the Greek word *heureka,* meaning "I have found it"—is reported to have been the word that Archimedes cried when he found a way to test the purity of Hiero's crown. My grandparents wouldn't have known the etymology of the word, but they would have felt it, the anticipation, as they waited along with the other immigrants from Russia to receive their allotments of land.

By all reports, when they arrived in this mixed-grass virgin prairie, although daunted by the task of clearing the land of its complex, ancient root system, they were enthralled by the shape and look of the land, and by the prospect that they could finally live a peaceful life in this remote place, far away from political chaos.

Those first two generations of my family are long gone now, but the history that shaped this region is not so easily erased. The lasting effect of Jefferson's grid can be seen as you drive through the countryside, and from the air—fields in different hues of greens, tans, and yellows, often in such perfect, regular squares that the land gives the appearance of a patchwork quilt.

My ancestors would not feel at home, I realize, in the current ecological times, when wilderness is loved and cultivated land is labeled as "disturbed." Where monocultures, like corn and wheat fields, are vilified, and polycultures, like restored prairies, are glorified. For them, it would be a world turned upside down.

I have a debt to pay to grass. My genetic line—the person that I am—survived because two ancient grasslands on two separate continents were irrevocably altered by my ancestors. The more I acknowledge that debt, the more I come to love the place where I'm from.

"Either all of earth is holy or none is," Wes Jackson wrote in *Becoming Native to This Place.* "Either every square foot deserves our respect or none does." Jackson continues:

> It is possible to love a small acreage in Kansas as much as John Muir loved the entire Sierra Nevada. This is fortunate, for the wilderness of the Sierra Nevada will disappear unless little pieces of nonwilderness become intensely loved by lots of people. In other words, Harlem and East Saint Louis and Iowa and Kansas and the rest of the world where wilderness has been destroyed must come to be loved by enough of us, or wilderness, too, is doomed.

A few years ago in a cartoon that appeared in *USA Today,* two men are sitting at a bar with frosty mugs of beer in their hands. One is looking at the other and saying, "You know, it's true. I've never met anyone from North Dakota *either*."

This statement would be funny, if it were not so true. I can't count the number of people I've met out in the world, most of them educated, diplomatic people, who have blurted out, "You're the first person from North Dakota I've ever met," as if I'm some exotic specimen, like Ishi, the last of his tribe.

Once, when I took my visiting brother to a dinner party in the small college town where I now teach, the woman who was seated beside him—a polished New Yorker, an ad exec who was visiting our hostess—turned to my polite brother and said, "You know, I've never met anyone so *rural* before."

My brother looked down at his lap and straightened his napkin. I felt like throwing my plate of moussaka at her. Perhaps I was overreacting, but it was the way she said the word *rural* that got me, as if it were some distasteful thing she regretted putting in her mouth.

But North Dakota *is* rural (I can say it because I'm from there) and largely invisible to the rest of the country. Cell phone reception in many parts of the state is still tenuous. As recently as ten years ago in certain places, my car radio would scan straight through the FM frequency without finding one good signal. Even Greyhound has abandoned us, recently discontinuing its routes through the state.

The only time the rest of the country pays attention to us is when some radical fringe group, like the tax-protesting Posse Comitatus, hidden away in our far recesses resists a string of warrants and blows away the FBI agents who come to arrest them. Then the networks follow up with a made-for-TV docudrama—usually entitled something like *Murder in the Heartland.*

In the 1980s, North Dakota commissioned a study to determine the state of the state. The findings, entitled *Vision 2000,* revealed that the state suffered from an acute lack of self-esteem. "We wanted to see what kind of an image people had of North Dakota," Kevin Cramer, the state tourism director, said, "and what we found was they didn't have one at all."

The study did find that people associated the word *north* with "cold" and *"flat"*—two images from which the state wished to disassociate itself. In 1989 and in 2003, the legislature proposed dropping the word *North* from *North Dakota* and simply calling the state *Dakota*. A headline in the *Wall Street Journal* asked, "Would a Rose Smell as Sweet If Its Name Was North Dakota?"

"It may sound ridiculous," the *Journal* article continued, "that a state riddled with towns named Zap and Judd and Gackle would say that its own name lacks warmth." The reporter solicited the assistance of Frank Delano, chairman of Delano, Goldman & Young, a New York City consulting firm responsible for renaming companies like Unisys and Navistar. "If North Dakotans want to present a warmer image to the world, Mr. Delano has another suggestion: Palm Dakota."

"You know, like Palm Springs," Mr. Delano said.

Most often North Dakota is famous for floundering at the bottom of national lists and for being the last state in the union to overrule archaic Wild West prohibitions like leaving your horse unattended, or obstructing views by wearing large bonnets at public places of amusement.

But what really hurt was the time a few years ago when Rand McNally, those conscientious mapmakers who so efficiently track every country in the world—Djibouti, Mauritania, Gabon—every changing border, every revised spelling of every new territory, neglected to include part of North Dakota in their *1989 Photographic World Atlas*. They left out parts of South Dakota and Oklahoma, too, but that didn't make North Dakotans feel any better. Having low self-esteem, we take these things personally. The *New York Times* article headline read, "Rand McNally Covers All 47 States."

"It was an editorial decision," Conroy Erickson, Rand McNally's public relations director said in response to heated inquiries. "Now that this has come up, we realize that it was not a good idea."

This list of grievances, slights against the good name of North Dakota, which reads like a foreshortened version of Luther's ninety-five theses, preys on the already fragile ego of every North Dakotan. We collect these episodes, licking our wounds in private, keeping obsessively detailed mental logs of these infractions, as those who are powerless tend to do.

In a 1990s episode of *TV Nation,* Michael Moore sent a film crew to North Dakota to investigate why the state is, according to U.S. Department of Commerce statistics, *the least visited state in the union.* By some stroke of luck, the reporter, Karen Duffy, managed to arrive in Fargo during a record snowstorm.

"Here we are at the Fargo International Airport," Duffy says, walking down a long, absolutely deserted corridor. "As you can see, this airport was specially constructed to handle the daily tide of tourists." The camera shows empty rolling escalators, a bored security guard at an abandoned screening station, and one lonely suitcase rotating endlessly on a luggage return carousel.

The report features protracted shots of long, stormy highways with nothing but the Doppler effect of a snowplow roaring past the camera. Duffy goes to the state capitol to interview then-governor Edward T. Schafer, who gets dewy-eyed when bragging about the inducements of the state—the solitude, for example.

"North Dakota is a place that you can get lost in," Schafer observes, as if that were a good thing. Then, not wanting to give the wrong impression, he clarifies, "I don't mean, lost on a map. I mean, you can really get lost *mentally* here." As if that was a good thing.

Duffy ends the report in Strasburg, North Dakota, polka dancing in the deep snow around the boyhood home of Lawrence Welk. This off-the-beaten-track tourist attraction, now a historically preserved North Dakota landmark, was part of a controversy in 1990 when President George H. W. Bush harshly criticized a $500,000 rural development grant passed by Congress to restore Welk's original homestead. The grant also included a provision to build a hotel in town to house the throngs of tourists who were sure to flock to Strasburg. Bush singled out the grant as the worst example of pork barrel politics he'd ever seen.

"I mean we all like Lawrence Welk," he said, bending his knees and making a little *oom-pa* motion, "but this is ridiculous." Bush, never a funny president, had the whole press corps laughing that day.

I'm sure even Lawrence laughed at this. He was still alive then, and he was a multimillionaire. As my father used to say when I made fun of Lawrence's corny accent, "He laughs all the way to the bank with that."

I don't recall anyone telling me that it was necessary to suffer for one's art, but instinctively I looked for it as a child. And on the Welk Show, it appeared to me that no creative demons were being exorcised, no addictions fought, no lust succumbed to or overcome, no one was struggling against the forces of censorship or racism. I believed that sweat poured from the brows of real performers who played on, oblivious to their audience. The Welk musical family seemed too aware of the camera, too eager to entertain me.

At an early age I had theories about musicians, especially singers, which I separated into two categories. On one hand were "singers," who sang nicely, in tune, enunciating every word. On the other hand were "vocalists," who massaged the musical line, the notes pouring from them like a fluid animal, the words becoming inconsequential. Vocalists could transport you to a place that was all blood and body memory.

As far as I could see, there were no vocalists on the *Lawrence Welk Show,* only milquetoast, third-rate nightclub singers. No one bordered on chaos, with the possible exception of Jo Ann Castle, a honky-tonk piano player, who didn't last long on the show precisely for that reason: Concerned viewers wrote in and complained that she played too many wrong notes. Even Arthur Duncan, an African-American tap dancer on the Welk show, seemed too manageably light-skinned.

Real players teased the melody, I thought. They rushed ahead, then hesitated, then let it out all at once. Welk's musicians played their lines a measure at a time, like conservatives tucking a little money away every week.

"Man, are they good!" my father used to exclaim. "Everybody on this show always looks so neat!" Small groan from me in the corner. But who could deny such success, my father argued, a weekly show on national television? "Come back and talk to me when you have your own show."

I remember the night in February 1964 when we all watched The Beatles together on *The Ed Sullivan Show.* My father fumed on the couch as the performance began, galled by the idea that anyone would pass off this noise as music. He retired to the bathroom in the middle of "She Loves You." It's funny to think now that my father suffered through all those Aqua Velva commercials, yet he chose one of the most significant moments in television history to go to the bathroom.

When he came back, The Beatles had finished their first set, and, appropriately, a commercial for Anacin headache tablets was on. Then the show resumed, and the Broadway cast of *Oliver!* featuring the future-Monkee, Davy Jones, took the stage.

"Thank god, that's over," my father huffed. "I flushed them down the toilet."

A few years ago, driven by morbid curiosity, I read Lawrence Welk's autobiography, W*unnerful, Wunnerful.* He learned to play the accordion from his father, an amateur who played around the county for wedding dances and other occasions. One summer when he was a teenager, Lawrence broke his leg and was unable to do farm work. He spent hours that summer practicing the accordion in the hayloft of the barn while his brothers worked in the fields.

In 1924, the morning he turned twenty-one, Lawrence Welk woke up before dawn. According to an earlier agreement he'd made with his father, he was now free to leave home and pursue his musical career. In *Wunnerful, Wunnerful,* Welk explained that he got dressed in an unfamiliar new suit that he had ordered especially for his departure.

> I inspected the contents of my valise one more time, and counted my small hoard of money. I had enough for my train fare plus three one-dollar bills, which I pinned in my inside coat pocket, and a little loose change. I smoothed the patchwork quilt, which my mother had made, over my bed for the last time, and then looked around the room where I had spent so many hours with my brothers. I felt no unhappiness, only a great eagerness to begin my great adventures.

"So you're going," Welk's father said to him from the breakfast table when he appeared with his suitcase. It's easy to visualize this scene, because the Lawrence Welk Museum display includes a dinner table perpetually set with family dishware.

"You'll be back," his father said to Lawrence that morning. "You'll be back just as soon as you get hungry."

"But I knew I would never return," Welk wrote. "I would never come back until I had proved myself."

On that day back in 1924, Welk went into Strasburg and boarded the train. He took it south, as far as his money would carry him—to Aberdeen, South Dakota, a mere 125 miles from his hometown, but no easy task considering the distances he had to cross.

We children of North Dakota are programmed for flight. We populate the cities of this country, living as expatriate small-town midwesterners. We grew up wild in the middle of nowhere with the nagging suspicion that life was certainly elsewhere. Even our parents encouraged us to flee in search of better opportunities. When grown, we scattered in a kind of diaspora, a phenomenon known as "outmigration." But we always feel the pull of our home ground.

A few years ago in Iowa, I went to a reading by Kathleen Norris, the author of *Dakota: A Spiritual Geography*. The auditorium was filled with displaced Dakotans, émigrés hungry for that feeling of connection to the place that Norris's book describes so beautifully.

The question-and-answer session that followed the reading was surreal, not your usual round of literary questions. "Aren't you Doc Norris's granddaughter?" one man raised his hand and asked.

"Yes," Norris replied.

"Well, he delivered me," the man announced.

Later, dozens of people who did not look like your usual poetry reading audience stood in line to get the author to sign copies of her book. The line progressed slowly because each person had to tell Norris where he or she was from, how their stories intersected. I understand this hunger for connection.

I like the fact that somebody somewhere knows who I belong to. On a recent visit home, I stopped at The Korner, the bar my sister manages. It was the afternoon, but the usual clientele were seated along the bar on high stools, swilling beers, watching a muted television.

One of them stared at me as I stood at the counter, waiting for my sister to emerge from the back room. "Aren't you one of the Marquart girls?" he asked.

"Yes," I demurred, feeling like a movie star, happy to be recognized.

"Let's see, which one are you?" he asked, considering the various attributes of my three sisters. He rubbed his whiskery chin, his beer belly crowning under the hem of his T-shirt. "Aren't you the one," he said finally, shaking his finger at me, "who was in college for so long?"

I blushed and looked down. "Yes," I admitted quickly. Thank God he hadn't identified me as the one who broke her father's heart by dropping out of college and joining a rock-and-roll band. "The college girl," I answered, eyeing the door for my sister. "That would be me."

But now his imagination was engaged. "You must have been really stupid," he said, taking a sip from his beer, "that you had to stay in college for so long."

We both laughed. I didn't even feel like punching him. It was classic North Dakota humor—self-deprecating, dark and down-turning. Where I come from, the smart kids get to stay at home and the stupid ones are sent away to college.

And everyone knows, too much college will only make you stupider. As Wes Jackson points out in *Becoming Native to this Place*, "The universities now offer only one serious major: upward mobility. Little attention is paid to educating the young to return home, or to go some other place and dig in. There is no such thing as a 'homecoming' major."

Although I am separated from them now, the people of my hometown, by different geography and experience, we understand each other. We were all raised under the rough tutelage of the Great Plains, a fierce and loving taskmaster.

That flat land, so barren and unforgiving, the land our grandparents acquired through the Homestead Act, was not the best farmland, as it turned out. According to Frank and Deborah Popper, two urban planners out of Rutgers, the Great Plains boasts "the nation's hottest summers and coldest winters, greatest temperature swings, worst hail and locusts and range fires, fiercest droughts and blizzards, and therefore its shortest growing season."

The Poppers have declared the settling of the Great Plains "the largest, longest-running agriculture and environmental mistake in United States history . . . an austere monument to American self-delusion." They have gone so far as to propose that the government buy up the land, relocate the people, and return the entire High Plains to its original prewhite state—a buffalo commons.

My great-grandparents and grandparents pitted their own strong wills against the unrelenting elements of North Dakota, and the testimony of their hard lives proves the Poppers some-what right: The settling of the Plains was, especially in the early days, a tragic experiment.

But we, the surviving generations who were raised on the slim margins of the place, have been forged into a hardy breed, requiring little, expecting less, able to survive anywhere.

And no matter how far from that uncompromising land we drift, a long, sinewy taproot summons us, always, home.

4

PRODIGAL DAUGHTERS

My blue-eyed brother was born into a family of green-eyed sisters. He lived and moved among us with the anointed brow of an only son. And perhaps that's why my sisters beat him so ferociously when Mom and Dad left us alone on Saturdays for polka night or work in town.

I don't count myself among the combatants, because I was the youngest girl, only six, and because of the vantage point from which I've carried the memory these forty years— watching the scene from the living room doorway.

It's dark. The lamps have been extinguished. The silent light of the TV screen casts a blue glow onto the hardwood floor. I see my three sisters in silhouette, circling my brother with their clenched fists raised. My brother cowers between them, covering his head with his arms.

But why did they beat him? Because he was different? Because he was too cute and wore short pants? I don't recall any bloody noses or broken bones. Not even a telltale scratch on our mother's immaculately polished wood floors. The blows must have been benign, and the skirmishes short, because our brother never fought back. He was gentle and sweet-natured, forgiving as Jesus under their fists. It was impossible not to love him—Nicholas, our boy-king, our tiny emperor.

His were the slender shoulders our farm rested on. Three generations of land ownership hung in the balance. When he came of age in the early 1970s, my brother moved to town and rented a small house with another farmboy Dirty dishes gathered in the kitchen sink. Crumpled-up beer cans collected in the garbage.

He grew his hair long, raced stock cars, played the electric guitar, enlisted in the National Guard. For a time, he joined a custom combining crew and traveled around the country harvesting the fields of strangers. My father was left at home, working his wheat fields alone.

Later, my brother worked at a body shop. Then he bought a gas station. Eventually he succumbed to my father's appeals for his return—exhausted, perhaps, from a life lived against the grain of Father's disapproval. Wasn't our brother's fate sealed from the moment of his birth? Instinctively, we girls always knew this, and I suppose in the end that's why my sisters beat him.

The year that I was forming in the womb, 1956, big things were happening in the outside world. Alfred Kinsey died, his groundbreaking work already completed. Allen Ginsberg published *Howl*. The first neutrino was produced at Los

Alamos. In Russia, my grandparents' country of origin, Stalin was dead and Khrushchev was denouncing him at the Twentieth Communist Party Conference.

It's sobering to think of how in-progress the world is before we enter it. We arrive in medias res, like a latecomer to a potluck, a sad bowl of potato salad in hand, after everyone has filled up on baked beans and bratwurst.

Arriving so after the fact, I became the mascot in family photographs, the one with the funny hat or the pigtails askew, the one with the turned-up nose, caught crossing her eyes. In the choo-choo-train photos my mother staged each year in front of the Christmas tree, I was always the clumsy caboose. While my siblings lined up in perfect ranks and smiled on cue, their four neat heads a uniformly descending staircase, I clung to my sister Jane's pant leg—a shortcake come-along, always falling down or walking out of the frame at the last moment. It seems even from the beginning, I was stepping out of line.

By some strange miracle, my father took a shine to me. In my early photos, I can see the tenderness in his hands as he holds me for my baptism picture, the delight in his eyes in the snapshot of my first step.

Maybe he just liked babies, maybe he sensed I would be his last, or maybe because my arrival coincided with my father's inheritance, the acres of rocky soil and mountains of residual debt attached to our family farm, perhaps these two events became entwined in his imagination. I became something by which he could measure his progress. As I grew stronger, so did his grip on the albatross. As I prospered, so did the farm.

What causes love? How do we ever deserve it? My father's favor, although never spoken, was always palpable. If we were kittens and our litter was threatened, I sensed my mother would be forced by biological imperative to save my oldest sister with her silken ponytail and my brother with his Y chromosome. I always knew my father would come for me.

There is a gravel road about a quarter-mile long leading out of my parents' farm that leads to another gravel road about a half-mile long that eventually meets up with Highway 3. When I was a kid, I sat for hours in my brother's bedroom facing the highway, and I kept a running tally of how many cars and trucks passed our farm—their color, make, model, and whether the vehicle was traveling north or south. I yearned for movement back then, for escape.

I spent a lot of time walking—restless, aimless pacing, down the gravel road, along the section lines, always kicking stones, walking with my head down, searching for some evidence that something had happened on this barren strip of land.

I drew maps with large X's on them, marking the spot where surely treasure would be found. I looked for chipped arrowheads, a stone carving, an agate, an unusual rock formation—anything to prove that someone or something, a nomadic tribe or an ancient glacier, had passed through before me, thereby proving it was possible to escape.

My three older sisters made their rapid getaways after they graduated from high school—the two oldest to college, the third to marriage and children in town. One by one, their belongings were packed into cars that disappeared down the gravel road. Their old bedrooms became my pick of bedrooms. Pretty soon I had the top floor of the house to myself, and I was left alone with my parents on that farm with so many chickens to feed, so many cows to milk, and so much land to work.

From sunup to sundown, my parents ran frantically from place to place trying to perform all the chores that kept the farm afloat. By then, they had sold their share of the bar, and the farm was our sole means of support. Since I was a teenager, and none of this had been my idea, I determined to make myself as useless as possible. The most my father could do was assign me small jobs from season to season.

One of my early chores on the farm was running the De Laval cream separator, a machine that worked its transforming magic in a cozy closet off the milk room. In this sanctum sanctorum ordinary milk was poured into a large, stainless steel bowl on the top of the whirring, spinning separator.

By some alchemy, the liquid filtered through the layers of the machine. After a great deal of noise and centrifugal gyration, the separator brought forth cream that flowed like gold from one of the spigots below.

From the second spigot appeared the now skimmed milk, which was quickly mixed back into the pot-bellied bulk cooler. Every few days, a driver arrived in our yard with a refrigerated tanker truck capable of siphoning from the cooler the many gallons of milk we extracted from our cows. This was taken to Wishek Cheese, a factory in a town about twenty-five miles southeast of Napoleon, where it was turned into curd, we were told, then shipped off to Wisconsin where it was worked into blocks, and aged. When it reappeared in our grocery store as Wisconsin Cheese only we were the wiser.

But the cream had choicer destinations. It was collected in pint and quart jars, each marked with the names of people in town who had ordered fresh farm cream. Mother hand delivered the jars the next day.

Of all the chores I had to do on the farm, I liked running the separator the best. The milk room was warmer than the rest of the barn, and my primary responsibility was to keep the cats away from the cream. I could take a book and read as the noisy machine churned and shook the life from the milk. Around me, things were filled and emptied; cream poured from spouts, jars were whisked away, and I was left to read my book hunched over in the dim light.

At my feet, tabbies and tomcats, tuxedos and calicos, milled and meowed. They craned their necks and howled with tortured voices. They tried to scale my pant legs, their claws out, just to get a quick paw, a stretched tongue, anything, into that golden stream. I would shoo and bat them away, absorbed in thought, clutching my book and reading all the while about all the strange places and marvelous people in the outside world.

I grew up in an almost bookless house, aside from the Betty Crocker cookbook and the gold-embossed row of *World Book* encyclopedias, which were only good for filling out the details in school reports. Great mysteries lurked out there in the world, I suspected, at which the *World Book* could only hint.

I read voraciously as a child, everything from Doctor Seuss to Nancy Drew. In the Catholic school I attended, the only books in the library, it seemed, were *The Lives of the Saints* and the *Baltimore Catechism*. The bookmobile saved me.

On Fridays, when the green and tan truck with the word *Bookmobile* painted across its length in bold letters pulled up to St. Philip Neri, we filed in threes from our classroom to the truck parked at the curb. I grabbed the safety bar and climbed the few steps taking in the smell of glue and old paper. I walked down the narrow aisle running my amazed fingers along the leather spines.

I imagined the gray-haired librarian who drove the bookmobile to be a secret hell-raiser, a madwoman for literature taking wild turns and careening around corners, the red velvet safety cords straining to hold the books in the shelves—all this fuss just to bring us heretical texts from the outside world.

I loaded myself down, negotiating the three descending steps with a stack of books taller than my eye level. Friday nights after the school bus dropped us off at home, I crawled into bed and read. I'd fall asleep with the smell of clean sheets and the comforting weight of books around me.

For all the books I read, it seems strange to admit now that I recall very few of their plots or details until I discovered the work of Carlos Castaneda as a teenager. Who in my small town could have recommended to me these books on Native American mysticism and psychotropic drugs?

I recall going to the Kirkwood Mall in Bismarck on one of our semi-annual shopping trips and asking the person behind the bookstore counter for anything by Carlos Castaneda. I felt nervous, as if I were requesting pornography, but he showed me to the shelf with *The Teachings of Don Juan: The Yaqui Way of Knowledge,* a book that chronicles Castaneda's apprenticeship with Don Juan Matus, an expert in medicinal plants and herbs, a Yaqui shaman and sorcerer knowledgeable in matters of personal power and all unseen matters. In the next few years, I would seek out more of his books—*Journey to Ixtlan, A Separate Reality, Tales of Power.*

When I think of myself as a teenager reading Carlos Castaneda in my upstairs bedroom, I wonder what I could possibly have understood of the world—seen or unseen? Yet when I look back at the actual copies of these books, I find that my underlinings and check marks were astute, that I recognized important passages when I read them: taking death as an adviser, stopping the world, finding your power spot, losing your personal history. I remember studying these lessons, willing myself to master them in my own life.

"It is best to erase all personal history," Don Juan advised, because that will make you free from the encumbering thoughts of other people. Don Juan explained that you strengthen the hold of your personal history by telling your parents, your relatives, and your friends everything you do, which locks you into a personal history that is binding. Instead, you must learn fluidity and mutability.

Little by little, Don Juan advised Castaneda on how to escape the limiting hold of personal history: "You must create a fog around yourself; you must erase everything around you until nothing can be taken for granted."

At thirteen, I remember how I pored over these passages late into the night with only the deep country darkness outside and the sound of crickets, fervently vowing to someday erase myself into the larger world.

Inspired by some stupid logic, I broke open a thermometer, freeing the mercury from its glass tube. No more would it be forced to serve, rising and falling encased in glass under our sick tongues. I kept the silver dollop of mercury in a saucer on my dressing table.

"I must be as cunning as quicksilver," I thought. At times when I wasn't reading Castaneda, I would roll the mercury around in my palm contemplating elusiveness. "I must learn to shape shift," I told myself, not realizing I could have been poisoning myself. Not that I would have believed it—if a snake had bitten me, I would have thought my will was powerful enough to survive its deadly venom.

I'd sit in my upstairs bedroom and jab at the drop of mercury, trying to pick it up, admiring the way it split and rolled into dozens of little pieces evading my silver fingertips.

If you're a young person growing up in the middle of nowhere, as I was, and you're not sure why the lottery of birth has landed you in this miserable locale, you begin to puzzle it out. Surely you were switched at birth and your real parents will soon be around to pick you up. Or perhaps you were flung through space in a small pod, ejected from some dying planet in a supreme act of sacrifice by your loving parents. After all, when Superman hurtled to earth, didn't he end up in the Midwest?

In the meantime, as your powers develop, cultivate incompetence. Perform chores so slowly that people will rush ahead of you to do them, or so badly that no one will ask you to do them in the first place. Incinerate the oats and feed the milk cows the garbage. Leave gates open. Let out the prize bull. Spill whole buckets of cream, and drive the new pickup too fast over rutted land. That way you might enjoy a nice life in the country.

Growing up on a farm, you see and do things you later wish you hadn't. I have castrated, for example—or rather, I have sat on top of a high, narrow corral, pressed tight the heaving flank of a bull calf with all the strength my legs could muster, looped and yanked his thick tail high in the air and to the side so that my father could come in and castrate.

I've seen the long-handled pincers at work, seen the Rocky Mountain oysters roll in the dirt like two dislodged eyeballs, glossy as pearl onions. I've known people who fry up these delicacies, sauté them in butter, and eat them like tender scallops. I've also known people who eat those turkey gizzards that float in pickling juices in five gallon jars on the counters of backwater bars, although I have not been one of those people.

If you stay in the Midwest long enough and you go to the right places, you'll encounter all kinds of stuff. I've seen manure, for example, in an amazing variety of colors and consistencies. I have sprayed it with a hose, swept it into gutters, scraped it, buried it, burned it, and shoveled it. I've been up to my bootstraps in it, shit threatening to suck me down as I tried to step through it, spreading straw with a pitchfork so that the cows could lie one more day in it.

I've seen it in pastures—huge cow pies sprouting mushrooms, amazing droppage buzzing with flies, full of grass, seeds, and maggots, or dried flat as a Frisbee along the trail. There's a certain shade of it, an orangish, mustardy yellow with an almost fluorescent glow, called *scours,* which is a signal that you probably have a very sick calf on your hands.

Clothing designers have embraced this color, reproducing it lately by some unnatural combination of dyes, and when I see it in stores in the shapes of fashionable blouses, sweaters, and pants, I can't help but think of my father standing in the calf shed, pointing to the troubling pile and then scanning the pen for the calf that's on its back, the calf with the scruffy coat, the calf with the emaciated, curving ribs.

In the milk barn, I have seen Holsteins go on happily eating their oats as they raise their tails and let loose shit with such force, shoot it like projectile vomit across the aisle of the barn, nailing another cow or some unlucky person who may be walking through the barn at that moment. To be around for cleanup after something like this has happened is to understand what chores are.

Perhaps separation became my special talent, because my father put me in charge of separating the calves from the cows when it was time to wean them from their mothers.

On that day, the cows were herded into the barn, their udders heavy with milk. As usual, they filed in and put their necks through the stanchions lining the barn. The slats were closed around their necks, to hold them in place during milking. But as they entered the barn, their calves were culled away and taken by me to a separate pen I had prepared for them with fresh straw in another part of the barn.

At first the cows don't realize what's happening. They move through the enclosures and gates in their docile way. They eat the oats put in place for them inside the stanchion. But once outside the barn, after milking, they begin to look around, to sniff, as if trying to recall something they've forgotten. They turn their long necks; they swish their tails. Nothing.

Then they begin to call out, low mooing, until the calves answer. The cows moo and moo in the direction of the calves' voices, and the calves bleat back. This goes on for hours. The crying becomes unbearable. The calves look so small in their holding pen. They stick their heads through the fence, their bodies shaking as they wail. They push their hungry voices toward their mothers' frantic calling: "Where are you? Where are you?"

"Here I am. Here I am."

The separation of an offspring from a parent. It's the most unnatural event. You feel cruel when you're the one enforcing it. On those days, I will myself not to think about it. I only know that it's my job to feed them. I step into the holding pen with buckets of the warm milk I've mixed from powder. Our farm depends upon the real milk the mothers produce. I must convince the calves to accept the substitute.

One by one, I take the bawling face of a calf into my hands and coax it toward the bucket of powered milk. I dip my fingertips in the milky liquid in the bucket, which rests hard-edged and shiny silver between my legs. I slip my wet fingers into the mouth of the crying calf. Eventually, the tongue begins to suck, from exhaustion and hunger and instinct—the soft sandpaper tongue, the little pricks of new teeth on my fingertips, the slurping as they finally dip their snouts into the bucket of milk.

As they drink, the calves cry and hiccough. I stroke the curls on their soft foreheads. One by one they stop crying as they are fed. One by one, they lie down in their new straw beds, stretching their long, downy necks, and sleep.

They quiet this way, one after the other, until all is silent in the calf shed. But the crying in the mothers' holding pen doesn't stop. It goes on through the night and into the next day, sometimes for hours, sometimes for days.

Chores. Even the word registers a feeling for the task at hand: "I've gotta go home and do chores." Never singular, always plural, a job that interrupts some fun you're having, then grows and grows and grows like polyps in an intestine. One syllable quickly spat out or yelled up creaky stairs, the word *chores* describes a job so unsavory that to spend the energy using two syllables means you'd probably never get around to doing it.

It's best to turn away from chores, pretend you didn't hear the call, hope someone else will do them, better to turn back to the softness and warmth of your own bed, back to the brush of cotton and the sweet downy smell of sheets, than to skitter across cold wood floors in the dark, pull on old clothes and worn smelly shoes, and go out into the drafty, shit-smeared places where chores are done.

I have been pulled from my bed in my white nightgown after I've disregarded my mother's first and second calls, my father's third call for chores. I have been taken down to the big backyard near the chicken coop to help with butchering the hens.

My mother has already started. She is cutting necks. My grandmother kneels beside her, also cutting. Between them is a growing pile of chicken heads, wall-eyed, astonished open beaks, the stunned crop of white feathers against the pink wavy flesh of fading combs.

My oldest sister Kate is galloping around the yard like the cloaked angel of death, snaring chickens with a long, wire leg-catcher. When she traps them by the ankle, they squawk wildly, trying to catch the ground with the other leg and run away until she lifts them in the air and hands them, wings flapping, feathers flying loose, over to the neck cutters. In this way, my sister is God today.

My second-oldest sister Elizabeth is retrieving the chickens from the headless places they have flown to. Around and around she runs, looking for the vivid sprays that will signal a chicken is nearby—blood rising in fountains on the white stucco walls of the chicken coop, blood bucking up against the trunks of cottonwoods, blood in soaked patches on the grass, the red iron smell of oxidization strewn across the dewy green lawn.

As the youngest girl, I stand on the edge of this slaughter, guarding the three loads of laundry my mother has risen early to wash, the whites now flapping on the line. My mother is quick with the knife; her blade is sharp. She places the chicken on the ground, pulls its wings back, and severs the neck with one quick motion. Without turning to look up, she throws the bird into the air as if to separate herself from the act, then she grabs another live chicken.

My grandmother kneels beside her moving more slowly. She cuts off the head then holds her hand around the chicken's neck, tilting it like a wine bottle she means to pour down to nothing. Under her knee, the chicken bumps and claws until all the electrical impulses that drive its muscles are finished. Beside her is a large red pool running down the hill. And so, it seems, there are at least two ways to butcher a chicken.

The water is already boiling in tubs up the hill in the barn where we go to pluck the feathers. Sitting in a circle, we grasp the upturned claws and dip the chickens in steaming water. The feathers come off in clumps and drop into a tub between us. The smell is complex—water meets wool meets vinegar meets dirt—like wet fur, like bad feet.

We pluck the strong wing feathers with their deep roots, and peel away the body's blanket of feathers. Then we rub the skin for the downy layer and pick away the tiny pinfeathers nestling inside the deep pockets of skin.

Across the yard, Mother is in the milk house with the burning candle. She is the fire woman singeing the plucked bodies as she passes them over the flame. The room smells of sulfur, the deep-caked odor of burnt hair and flesh. Grandmother sits beside her, on a stool in front of the sink. She is the last one to receive the bodies, cutting them in a way that only she knows.

Grandmother places the chicken on its back before her. She opens the bird's legs looking for the soft spot unprotected by bone. "The behinder," she says, "the pooper," "the last part to go over the fence." She repeats these words all day again and again to keep us from fainting.

She draws a sharp blade across the film of skin between the legs. A world of steaming darkness spills out into which she must thrust her hand extracting the long weave of intestines, the soft gray lungs, the heart, the liver, the tiny green row of developing egg yolks, the brown gizzard all swimming in a gelatinous ooze. Carefully she finds the small sac of bile, the green-black poison that, if ruptured, will ruin the meat of the bird, and she cuts it away.

Only she knows how to distinguish the edible from the throwaway parts. She crops the feet from the body with a hard crunch of her knife and trims away the claws, the dirt still packed tight under the nails from the chicken's constant scratching for food. We recoil when she places the trimmed yellow feet on the edible pile. (She'll take them home in a bag to Grandfather at the end of the day, and we have no idea what they do with them.)

And when she holds the gizzard in her palm like a warm bun and draws a blade along the edge, turning the sac inside out to show us the chicken's last supper, I expect to see bottle caps, shiny pennies, diamond rings inside, but I find only an undigested clump of oats, a few tiny bits of gravel.

At the end of the day, we tuck in the wings and legs, slipping the naked birds into the dozens of water-filled milk cartons my mother has been saving all year for freezing the meat. She sets aside four of the biggest birds for frying that night.

"Mmm, girls," she says, "just think—fresh chicken."

"Ughh," I say to Grandmother as we walk the red wheel-barrow to the dump ground to bury the parts, the metallic tinge of blood still in my mouth.

"Do I really have to eat it?" I ask. I could use a few days for amnesia to set in. But Grandmother tells me I must. I must learn to know the taste of what my hands have done on my tongue.

I did a tough apprenticeship in storytelling with my family, sitting around the supper table where we seven ate our meals together. On Sundays or holidays, our grandparents would join us, and our numbers would blossom to ten or twelve. The platters of roast beef, mashed potatoes, fried chicken, and dumplings would go around, tipping precariously as they were passed from hand to hand. The food was always less important than the talk, and the thread of the story always held firm over any interruptions.

Eventually the empty platters came to rest in the center of the table as people leaned back in their chairs. No one got up to put away leftovers—we didn't worry then about botulism or the dreaded salmonella. The stories took on a full head of steam. We were small people, but we were big talkers, and the best talker of all was my father. He was mercurial. If you wanted to rise up over the arc of his narrative, you had to throw in something big and surprising.

And not only did it have to be inventive, but it had to be relevant, because the members of my family could be bru-tal. If you added something that didn't contribute to the momentum of the story, someone was likely to turn to you and say, "And your point would be?" or "And you're telling us this because?"

Some of my father's liveliest stories centered on my early attempts at driving, which usually ended with someone coming to my rescue—my father or brother running home to get the front-end loader or a bigger tractor to pull me out of the ditch or the muddy place where I'd gotten the tractor stuck. One too-tight turn on the way home with the loaded trailer, and the whole pyramid of bales toppled into the ditch. But no matter how bad my driving got, my father never tired of throwing the keys in my direction.

Fetching is a thing you do a lot of on the farm. The word *fetch* derives from the Middle English word, *fetchen,* and an Anglo Saxon word, *feccan,* meaning, "to bring." Despite its archaic sound, it's a well-used term on a farm.

One summer when I was a teenager, it was my job to fetch the milk cows each afternoon from the adjacent pasture where they'd been grazing all day. At 4:30, I was to get into the pickup and drive the half-mile to the pasture. I didn't mind this chore. It gave me a chance to sneak an afternoon cigarette in an otherwise smokeless household.

Once I reached the pasture, I would untie the long wire gate and pull it clear to the side, then drive into the pasture and circle the herd. As soon as I honked the horn, the cows would begin to move toward the open gate, already feeling the heaviness in their udders. They ambled along, following an old animal trail that had probably been there before the pasture and the fence, before me and the pickup had ever made an appearance on this land.

I idled behind them as they made their slow way. I lit a cigarette and sucked in the swirling smoke, feeling the satisfying nicotine expand into my lungs. I listened to the radio and sang "In-A-Gadda-Da-Vida" at the top of my lungs.

Was it some new scent, some passing distraction, that caused about fifteen of the cows to fork off one day, to turn down an intersecting road and move slowly in another direction away from the farm? This made me mad. I honked the horn, yelled "hey, hey, hey." I pounded on the roof of the pickup to draw them back to the herd, but they continued to move away.

I got out of the pickup, leaving it running in the middle of the intersection. I picked up some gravel and ran down the road, throwing rocks and cursing at them.

And just as they began to turn around and make their way back, I heard a loud noise behind me—the metal *kerchunk* of bumper meeting grass meeting fence post. When I turned to look, I saw the pickup had already come to rest, the front end was lodged impossibly against the corner post, and the back end was dug into the soft shoulder of the ditch.

Underneath the pickup's jammed frame, from where I stood, I could see the deep curve of the ditch. I knew that backing it out was not an option for me. Then I did what any farm kid does in this situation—I swore first, then I began to run home fast. As I was running, I looked up the road to the house and saw my brother and father already coming out of the front door with the keys in hand for the tractor that would pull me out of the ditch.

After the dust of that day settled, this would be a story my father told again and again. He told it to Grandma and Grandpa, he told it to friends I brought home from school, to boyfriends I brought home from college.

He said he'd been watching me that day through the binoculars, and that he'd actually seen the pickup roll in the ditch behind my unsuspecting back. He had watched the horror dawn on my face as I turned to discover the pickup in the ditch, and he had observed my anguish as I took off running toward the farm.

According to him, I had run so fast that day that I passed the milk cows—the older ones, the pregnant ones, the younger ones—I made my way through the ranks, even lapping our German Shepherd–Collie mix, Tippy, who had been racing down the road wild-tongued beside me.

Eventually, he said, the only thing in front of me was a rabbit that had been flushed from the ditch. It was running scared in long, scalloping lopes, but when I came upon it, I kicked it in the ass and said, "Get out of the way and let somebody run who knows how to run." That's how fast I was going.

What could I do but suffer through this story time and time again? For my father chose to leave out the one incriminating detail, the burning cigarette that he and Nick most certainly must have found smoldering in the ashtray when they pulled the pickup out.

But he never mentioned the cigarette because that would have ruined the story. Then it would have become a "cigarette in the ashtray" story, rather than another good story about the time Debbie drove a vehicle in the ditch. Maybe he knew that withholding the most tender secret in a story makes the telling all the more delicious.

There at that supper table I learned to listen. As the youngest child, I was at play in a field that everyone around me had long ago mastered. But listeners have their place in stories as do laughers, a job my grandmother took on. Without listeners and laughers, stories have nowhere to live. They float away and are forgotten.

Sometimes it's hard to pin down a family story. They shift before you like mirages. A few years ago, my mother told me about the day my brother Nick came home from school—he was maybe ten—and as soon as he stepped off the bus, he took his Tonka truck to the garage and smashed it flat as a hub cab with a hammer. What had warranted such violent behavior, my mother still sometimes wondered.

I filed this away and asked my brother the next time I saw him. "What was the deal with the Tonka truck," I asked. "What made you so mad?"

"I didn't do that," Nick said. "Jane did that."

Interesting strategy, I thought. Blame it on the sister. Some time passed before I remembered to tell my mother what I had learned. "Nick says he didn't smash the Tonka truck," I told my mother. "He says Jane did it." I waited for my mom's definitive reply.

"What Tonka truck?" my mother said with a perplexed look. By then, she had forgotten the entire episode. So you have to keep an eye on family stories, lest they fall through the crack between the two worlds.

Here's one thing I remember for certain: I only saw my father cry once. It was the morning my brother left home the first time. He was eighteen and had just graduated from high school. They had been arguing that morning in the barn while doing chores. I remember waking to the sound of loud voices, followed by the rumble of my brother's hot rod muffler and his tires throwing gravel as he peeled out of the yard.

My first thought was that there had been some terrible accident. I threw on my shoes and ran out to the yard in my pajamas. All was silent except for the rhythmic suction of the milking machines coming from the barn. I crossed the yard and approached the barn slowly. Through the open door, I saw the rows of cows swishing their tails.

When I got closer, I peered inside the door, afraid of finding spattered blood, some evidence of a disaster. But I saw only my father. He was leaning against the support post weeping, his face covered with his hands.

A few years later as a teenager, when I was feeling my wildest oats, I decided to run away from home myself. My three older sisters were long gone, and my brother hadn't yet been summoned home from his adventures. I had argued with my father that afternoon about a wrestling match going on in town. I wanted a ride, but he needed me to stay at home and help with chores.

I remember stomping across the yard and throwing on a red barn coat for the three-mile walk to town. It wasn't my coat, and red wasn't a color I often wore. But I remember the episode so vividly because of the red coat, and because of the way I imagined my father's eyes would follow me—a defiant crimson mark on the flat horizon, making small progress away from him, then disappearing as the road curved by the wildwoods and dipped into town.

I stayed at a friend's house that evening and bummed a ride home in the morning. My father greeted me in the yard on his way to the barn for chores.

"So you're back." He chuckled and handed me a bucket as my friend's car circled our drive and roared away down the gravel road. "You can start by feeding the chickens."

Sure, it would have been nice if he'd rejoiced, called the neighbors over, and killed a fatted calf upon my return. But I'd only been gone for twelve hours, and I hadn't yet wasted my substance with riotous living, as the parable requires. Besides, fatted calves were reserved for prodigal sons, even I knew that.

At the very least, I thought, he'd gotten the message. I wouldn't be hanging around this dust hole forever.

5

THE HORIZONTAL LIFE

On the flat horizon of a midwestern town, the grain elevator props up the whole sky; it holds down the earth. The grain that sleeps fat and finished inside the elevator comes from sunshine and soil. It brings together heaven and earth.

The railroad tracks that pass by the elevator crisscross the country. They sew together the land in great, long stitches connecting the people in the small towns to larger cities and the grain to shipping ports.

The day the grain elevator burned down in my hometown, the people gathered to watch it smolder and explode in blue billows and flames. "What catastrophe," they murmured. All those connections were reduced to ashes. The town felt cut off from the rest of the world.

As the blaze gained strength, the volunteer firemen trained their hoses on the hottest parts of the spire and circled the elevator. They would not be made to do anything heroic, even though it was their own carefully cultivated grain surrendering itself to the flames.

Perhaps it was a spark, some friction in the dust, or a carelessly discarded cigarette that started the elevator burning, but now it was the very substance of the grain that sustained the original spark, still to be found somewhere in the larger context of the blaze, growing from yellow to orange to red, roaring up and crackling in a way that the tiny spark couldn't have imagined.

She would never have lost her virginity—the girl that I was—if the grain elevator had not burned down. She was not your stitch-in-time-saves-nine kind, not your roll-the-extra-string-into-a-ball-and-save-it type of young woman that fiction writers who write stories about midwestern girls like to create.

If you had to classify her, you would say that she was a spender, that she was all thin limbs and long hair, that she was fourteen years old and she had that walk down cold—the walk of someone who does not believe in life after twenty.

Not that she was saving her virginity for anything special. In fact, she saw it as a filmy substance, a dying skin that needed to be cast off. At that moment, fire appeared as rescuer, as change agent.

How intensely it burns and how little it leaves the girl that I was thought while watching the grain elevator burn down. It reminded her of the cigarettes her busy sister lit and left unsmoked in the ashtray, the thin column of ashes burning clean down to the filter.

Already she has an eye for metaphor that will only cause her problems. This habit of drawing equations between unlikely objects, an ability that will serve her so well later in life, only meets with raised eyebrows and shakes of the head in this small town.

The grain elevator burning down will prove to be a symbolic event in her life, not that the girl that I was would have perceived it as such, since she had never heard of symbols and will not hear about symbolism for a good many years—long after she had ceased to be herself and was well on her way to becoming someone else who would, by some strange twist of fate, become me.

At this point in her life, she's working on more basic concepts—small things like trying to get people to call her Deb, instead of the more childish Debbie, and trying to find someone to lose her virginity to.

By the time we see her here, she has experienced a number of things. She's tried French kissing and seen plenty of window fog. She's had her breasts nibbled, studied, and stroked. She's explored an endless variety of back seats, quietly undoing snaps and zippers and tricky belt buckles, slipping her hand deep into the moist pants of a local boy. The horizontal life has not completely eluded her.

But she has impossible standards. She does not want the tentative touch of a novice, nor does she want a clumsy farm boy. No one who wears tidewater plaid pants, smells of cow manure, and lusts more for her father's full six quarters of land than for her own strong, slim, and tanned body.

She's no longer interested in shy exploration, or wonder-ment, or handing her carefully pruned virginity over to a husband on a wedding night. She has an itch somewhere deep inside her, in a place she cannot even begin to direct someone to. But she doesn't want it scratched, she wants it vanquished. It will take an expert, someone who is as efficient as he is kind. She's looking for a wolf with a nice demeanor. But whoever this guy is, if he ever lived in this town, has cer-tainly moved away.

So, discontented, this girl that I was gathers with the rest of the people of her town lined along the railroad tracks and watches the grain elevator flare with fire and disappear in a dark plume of smoke.

Fire loves me; in my youth, it so marked me as its own. Fire in my head like exploding stars, my first memory. Three years old, a ring of fire burning in my vision. First, it broke through the curtain of my sight—a grove of chokecherry trees, a field of alfalfa bales, white sheets flapping on the line, my father's hand grasping a milk bucket—all that I saw solid before me dissolving into fragments.

It began with flashing shimmers of light in the shape of a V in the center of my vision. Then it grew over the next hour, adding more shimmering V's around the periphery of my eyesight. Within moments, the shimmering V's joined into a circle and spread, dissolving my vision into a blind wash of light. The world around me became slashes of light reflecting back to me in fragments like the shards of a broken mirror.

The first time it happened, I was in the backyard helping my sister Elizabeth feed the chickens. We were slinging oats from a sack in wide arcs onto the ground. We were like the sower in the Van Gogh painting, with the orange disc of the sun pelting golden droplets of sunlight on us as we pelted the earth with golden droplets of oats.

The chickens rushed at us in excitement, so plump and so white. Their wild feet clawed the ground as they ran—two hundred clucking white chickens running at us in the bright sunshine—and that's when the V of shimmering light broke through my vision for the first time.

I tried to breathe. The green of the fresh cut grass felt ripe in my throat; the sun glared in my eyes. Even in the cool morning air, I grew feverish, sweaty. I bent over to escape the light, but when I closed my eyes I still saw it, the explosion shimmering in my head.

Something inside my stomach felt too large, something had to come up. My sister held me from behind so that I wouldn't throw up on my clothes. I was the youngest; she was the second-oldest. If I made a mess, she would have to clean me up. She knew how I hated water, how I kicked and screamed under the sink on Saturday nights when she and my oldest sister tried to wash my hair for church the next morning. So my sister Elizabeth held my hair out of my face as I got sick, the fire in my head blazing for the first time.

I had problems swallowing as a child, and breathing some-times, too. At a nervous moment, I'd convince myself that I would never swallow again. Saliva would gather in my mouth.

"Oh no," I'd say to myself. "I'll have to go through life, spitting and spitting." Then I would get distracted and swallow naturally, and the crisis would be over until the next time.

And there were breathing problems. I could never get a deep breath. I'd yawn, pop my ears, panic for air, gulp and gulp and gulp, until my sisters would turn and complain, "Dad, she's doing it again." Then my dad would bend down, get his red face right next to mine, and scream, "Now, you just relax," which always resulted in a deep intake of breath.

In addition to the breathing and swallowing problems, I had other nervous foibles as a child. I was overly concerned with the edges of carpets. I imagined they had invisible safety fields that rose to a height of one or two feet around their fringed borders. So you couldn't just lazily step onto a carpet, no, you had to high-step your foot onto it, so as not to trip the invisible laser beam that guarded the rug's edges.

I was worried about what hid under the furniture. I believed that all of my dead grandparents slept in a tight group under my bed, which gave me some trouble with sleep.

For a while as a teenager, I had skin rashes, great flaking patches of psoriasis on my elbows and at my hairline. I had an excitable mind that rushed from subject to subject. At some point, I would stop myself and say, "Wait, how did I get to this thought?" Then I would try to think backwards—this thought led to that thought which led to this other thought, etc. But I could never make my way back to the original thought.

Before I had words to describe it, the ring of fire took over my field of vision. The blurry eye, I came to call it. "Mom, can you come and get me," I'd learn to call my mother and ask. "I've got my blurry eye." Stress triggered it; food triggered it; later hormones triggered it. But people became suspicious of my blurry eye. It would happen so suddenly—one moment I'd be talking and laughing in a group, then the next minute, I'd be ashen, saying, "I have to go. I've got my blurry eye."

In time, I would learn I had twenty minutes to get to a safe, quiet place before the light blinded me. I'd learn to avoid all smells, especially food smells, even though my mother always seemed to be baking bread or slow-cooking a plump, juicy roast on the days when the blurry eye came. The acid smell of food would line my throat. The bathroom light where I would go to shake aspirin out of the bottle blinded me. The sound of my sisters' laughter in the next room wounded me. The flannel blanket grated on my skin.

Migraines, eventually my grandmother explained. Inherited from her—she would admit with guilt in her voice. Only she knew how to comfort me. Most times when they started, I would walk the five minutes to her house from school. She'd put me in a dark bedroom and wrap a tight washrag around my head, then sit on the side of the bed with me, talking quietly in the darkness as we waited it out. After the flashing lights dissolved in my field of vision, then the pain of the migraine started for real—hot-pokered anvils beaten to flatness inside my head.

There she is, the girl that I was, the year before the grain elevator burned down. She's thirteen. Her profile is flatter, her hair straighter, but still it's the same girl.

She's mowing the lawn on the Fourth of July. See how immaculate are the lines she is making on her parents' dried-up lawn? The rows are perfect, like a landing strip she is preparing for someone who may be passing overhead.

Already she is scanning the horizon for methods of escape—light aircraft, men in goggles with long scarves streaming behind them. Already she is scheming quick passage out of this dust hole, this graveyard that her father inherited from his father, inherited, in turn, from all the fathers who came before.

Looking at the sky and thinking so intensely of flight, she feels the first jagged stab of menstrual pain crack at her navel and bury itself deep in her pelvis. She doesn't bother to go inside and find out what's happened. She understands the ever-widening stain that now spreads through her layers.

Instead, she keeps on working, looking only as far ahead as the expanse of her parents' lawn, concentrating on finishing another long row before the afternoon sun rises too high in the sky.

Later inside the house, she finds the cache of pads in the cupboard above the bathtub. Over the years she has watched this giant blue box empty and fill, empty and fill, never understanding until this moment the true significance of all this mysterious activity. Later after supper is eaten and the sun has disappeared, the girl gathers with the rest of her family on the newly mown lawn to watch the fireworks.

Her grandparents bring their folding chairs; her father brings his cooler. Her mother spreads a blanket, and her brother—who is going through a teenage boy phase, inspired by the space program, that makes him yearn to light, inciner-ate, and explode things into the sky—acts as official torch bearer, igniting bottle rocket after bottle rocket, shooting star after shooting star into the still night air.

As fountains of light hiss, spit, and transform into streams of gold in the sky, then fan into shapes of exotic flowers, the girl that I was lies down in the cool grass with her sisters and oohs and aahs in appreciation.

The summer after the grain elevator burned down, it began to rise slowly out of the ashes with the help of young work-men who appeared in the small town as if by magic.

They were tanned and rough-skinned.

Their hair was thick and dry as straw from the sun.

They were from another part of the state.

Mmm. The farmgirls savored the thought. *Fresh blood. New gene pool.*

The young workmen came to town with names like Leroy and Dale, Jimmy and George. They had cigarette packs stuffed in the pockets of their denim work shirts or bundled in the sleeves of their white T-shirts.

They had rugged jaw lines and razor stubble. They drove pumpkin orange Mustangs and convertible GTOs with earthquake stereos and Richter-breaking mufflers. They had piss-warm cases of Schlitz in the trunks of their cars.

Every day the people of the small town crossed the railroad tracks on their way from the courthouse to the bar or from the church to the store. As they passed the construction site, they stopped to watch the workers move on the girders of the newly emerging structure. Every day the girl that I was passed the elevator and watched the men pound in nails with their tanned, muscular arms.

One of the workmen was a lanky Nordic type. He was well into the sky when she first saw him. He was dangling on the ledge of a girder, a leather safety belt strapped to his waist, his thick yellow hair blowing in the wind.

He cut a striking figure up there with the sun blazing behind him, like a phoenix rising. The moment could be highly allusive. But it would be a mistake to assume that the girl that I was saw him as anything other than shirtless, big-armed, and well tanned.

Perhaps it was that walk of hers, that careless mad march that attracted his attention. She was crossing the railroad tracks on the way to her grandmother's house (this is no joke, she really was going to visit her grandmother) when she heard his whistle come from high above. She looked into the glare and saw only the flash of his white, white, very white teeth.

One of the things the girl that I was enjoyed doing with her friends was drive around. They'd pile in their cars and pass by other young people from their small town who were also driving around. They'd nod once, or lift an index finger from the steering wheel to acknowledge each other as they passed.

The Main Street of their small town was three blocks long bordered by a city park, which ended in a u-turn. As the young people busied themselves driving around on Main Street, they'd wave at each other coming and going. Then they'd make the u-turn and wave at each other again going and coming. Eventually, they'd get bored with this and angle park their cars in front of the Rec Hall.

One night, at the Rec where everyone went to play pool, smoke cigarettes, and eat the biggest orders of twenty-five-cent French fries in town, the girl that I was met up with the lanky workman from another part of the state.

His name was George, although he was no dragon slayer. He came to town in a two-toned blue '56 Chevy with no reverse gear and very little left of first. He was terrified of heights, but he was even more afraid of poverty, so he overcame his bad nerves each day, climbing the scaffolding, weak-kneed and hung over, rising higher and higher in the sky as the summer progressed.

She got close enough to notice that his breath smelled of spearmint, for he chewed gum liberally, flipping it around in his mouth with his tongue as he spoke, chattering away about something she did not understand because she was concentrating so exclusively on the length and shape and firmness of his thighs.

He had showered and changed. His hair was bleached and damp, and his skin was rosy from the sun. He wore a yellow shirt stripped open to his navel, revealing a nest of burnished chest hair. Perhaps this George, this elevator man, reminded her of a Viking marauder as he laughed and stroked his mustache. His lamb chop sideburns were dark and wispy, trailing down the sides of his face. When given the opportunity to browse, the girl that I was thought, she was certain to find every conceivable color of hair on this man's body.

They talked, but they talked of nothing, George and this girl that I was, for they had no common words with which to work. All they had were grunts and laughs, gestures and sighs, and fragments of words that they'd heard and vaguely understood, which they offered now to each other, peppering the silence that hung between them.

When he began his little dance, those circuitous steps he felt obliged to do to get her into his car, it came out seamless, a blending of feigned shyness, sly innuendo, and a fair amount of chest pounding.

That night in the Rec Hall, she watched this George, this second-story man, do his little dance knowing that it was not necessary, that it was never necessary for her sake, but allowing it to continue, recognizing, in her characteristic early wisdom, that it was necessary for him to do.

As they cruised Main, he smiled at her with his immaculate wide grin and fiddled with the radio. She studied the leathery quality of his large hands, wanting more than anything to trace with her finger the smooth line of his distinctive nose—the shape of which, when she encountered it later in life on the faces of other men, she would come to call an intelligent nose.

Riding along in this two-toned '56 Chevy with no reverse gear and very little left of first, the girl that I was did not think about trailer courts, or dirty dishes piled in the sink, or babies crying late into the night. She was lighting a cigarette, bending the tip deep into the flame. And when the ash grew long on the tip, she didn't flick it. She leaned back, just leaned back in complete repose.

And even though he was a stranger in town, she didn't bother to give him directions. So confident was she that he would find a way to get them wherever this girl that I was wanted to go.

Eventually as teenagers, we discovered uses for the land that did not involve work. Wild nights, we partied and parked in the moraine, the low glacial hills that run in a ten-mile-wide belt north of my hometown.

On summer weekends after the work was done, we drove up and down the hills, coming to park deep in the moraine beyond the reach of the law. Rows of cars lined up along the rim of the hills. Dozens of lovers went to those cars for privacy or took blankets and went out, deeper into the country for sex on the land.

Thousands of years ago in this spot, the Wisconsinan glacier dropped mounds of ice and the last of its chewed-up boulders and receded north toward the Hudson Bay as if suddenly intrigued by work in other quarters. The moraines that formed consist of rough belts of glacial hills that run like a diagonal line through the state of North Dakota. One of the moraines skirts the northeast edge of my family's farm as it goes through Logan County.

As teenagers, we understood nothing of the deep geological history of our family land. During the day we knew these morainic hills only from planting and harvesting, each ridge remembered in our bodies from long hours of strain and sweat. The rocks the glacier left behind were a nuisance that had to be cleared year after year as they surfaced.

But in the ravines of the moraine on summer weekends, we tapped kegs, lit bonfires. We danced around the flames that flared fifteen feet tall. Car doors were thrown open, stereos blared, women laughed in the night, the body opening with alcohol, the sweet forgetting that spreads through the brain.

The land lay around us like a telluric body, protecting us with its silence, its impassive largeness. The land loved us in our youth; it would never reveal to our parents what we had done in its presence.

In *The Myth of the Eternal Return,* Mircea Eliade noted that references to agricultural mysticism can be traced back to Greek myth: "Demeter lay with Iasion on the newly sown ground at the beginning of spring. The meaning of this union is clear: it contributes to promoting the fertility of the soil." Similarly, James Frazer noted in *The Golden Bough* that people in many ancient cultures engaged in sex on the land to create "the sympathetic influence of the sexes on vegetation."

In this view, sex is a blessing to the land, which encourages the forces of creation. Those bonfire nights on the moraine, drinking, dancing, lying together on the land: Did we realize we were engaged in an ancient ritual, an act of agricultural mysticism that would promote the fertility of our parents' land? Not at all. We were just horny teenagers.

Even on the continent of Europe, Frazer admitted, vestiges of similar rites still existed that could be seen as stunted relics of agricultural mysticism. In the Ukraine, the priests came to bless the fields then instructed the young married couples to lie down on the sown field and roll down the hills. In the early 1900s, the same practice of rolling down slopes together after the blessing of the land could still be found in parts of England.

In Russia, Frazer explained, the priest himself laid down in his long robes and vestments and rolled with the couples. If he was reluctant to do so, the participants urged him on, imploring, "You do not wish us to have corn, although you do wish to live on our corn." Here the relationship between human sexuality, fertility of the land, and productivity of crops is clear.

Our rude forefathers, Frazer wrote, "personified the powers of vegetation as male and female." Joining their bodies to the land in the act of sexual intercourse, they attempted, "on the principle of homeopathic or imitative magic, to quicken the growth of trees and plants."

In Amboyna, Frazer noted, cultural anthropologists observed that the clove farmers went naked into the fields at night when they feared the harvest would be inadequate, and they ejaculated on the trees, shouting "More cloves! More cloves!" And the husbandmen of Java had sex in the fields with their wives to encourage the bloom on the rice fields.

The Pipiles of Central America kept apart from their wives until the planting then indulged their passions, even appointing members of the tribe to perform the sexual act at the moment the seeds were planted. Frazer reported that the Nabataeans, "when grafting the branch of one tree onto another, would choose a maiden to insert the graft while she, in turn, was approached from behind by a male member of the tribe, who inserted himself into her to emulate the graft."

Frazer concluded, "The marriage of the trees and plants could not be fertile without the real union of the human sexes." These charms and rituals, he explained, were intended to encourage "the woods to grow green, the fresh grass to sprout, the corn to shoot, and the flowers to bloom."

Here lies the mythic essence of husbandry, the core of agricultural mysticism. By making love on the land, the husbandman symbolically marries himself to the earth in a binding contract. The couple's union blesses the land, ensuring the fertility of the crops. Children are produced from the union that takes sustenance from the fruit, corns, and grains. The fruit feeds upon the fruit. This arrangement ensures that the land will have a caretaker and that the caretaker will have a home. At the end of their lives, the cycles of generations are returned to the earth to provide sustenance to the land.

But what about the girl that I was, the daughter of agriculture who refused to be seeded or planted? *I will lie down on my father's land and rise up with nothing but my pleasure to show for it.*

By choosing pleasure over fertilization, I fear I have committed an act of extravagance that separates me irrevocably from the long line of agricultural women in my family.

It's not that I lied exactly; it's just that I was in possession of certain information that I did not disclose the night I was sixteen and the inside of my mom and dad's car burned down. It was the first night of my first job, and my mom had announced that I could take the car, instead of the pickup, which I normally drove to school events.

I was nervous as I dressed for my first day of work at Maggie's, the main restaurant in town situated at the intersection where Highway 3 passed by the grain elevators. I slipped into my red and white waitress uniform; I polished my white shoes. It was a warm fall afternoon and I was looking forward to having a real job where I would receive real pay.

By sixteen, I had already quit smoking, but I bummed a cigarette from my sister's pack, thinking it would calm me down on the ride to town. Once on the road, I lit the cigarette, but I quickly realized I no longer liked the taste of it.

My parent's blue Chevy had one of those virgin ashtrays that had never seen an ash, much less the searing tip of a cigarette butt. So I cracked open the window, tossed out the almost unsmoked cigarette, sealed the window, and cruised into town parking my car in the lot across from Maggie's, directly below the towering grain elevators.

The cook who greeted me at the door had worked Maggie's night shift for almost thirty years—she was a lifer with thick, grease-smeared glasses. She took me under her wing, as she must have done for hundreds of girls before me, showing me where the break room and the time clock were. Maggie walked me around the café, going over the menu, showing me how the cash register worked.

I was starting to get the hang of it three hours into my shift. There was a rhythm you could catch, an unstoppable flow that allowed you to sequence out the orders—delivering the daily special, the steak and potatoes, the hamburgers and cheeseburgers, the fries and shakes, all the while checking back to deliver bills and fill cups of coffee in between.

The tables were starting to thin, I noticed, but the restaurant was full. People had begun to leave their seats and collect at the front of the café where a large plate glass window faced the grain elevator parking lot. But I was a professional. I had many refills to pour. I would not be distracted away from my appointed tasks.

Eventually, the tables were deserted. All the customers were standing by the window, their coffee cups turning cold at their tables. They were staring at something going on across the street. I noticed then a flashing red light strobing over their heads as they milled around.

I moved closer, peeked through an opening between them and could just make out my parents' car in the parking lot across the street with all four doors thrown open. A fire engine was parked at a crazy angle beside it, as if they had rushed to the scene. Firemen were standing on either side of the car, hosing down the smoldering interior.

"My car!" I screamed, and all the customers parted to the side for me. I rushed through the opening, out the door and across the street just in time to watch a fireman, on his knees, pull one charred cigarette butt from between the exposed molding of what had been our blue Chevy's backseat.

"Looks like a cigarette," the fireman said to his partners. Then he looked at me. "This your car? Looks like somebody threw a cigarette in here." I glanced in the back seat. The wiring was completely exposed, and it was still sparking and fizzing.

The firemen left after they'd sufficiently extinguished the car, and I walked across the street to Maggie's to call my mom

and dad. I blubbered over the phone about the car and a cigarette, and some sparking electrical wires in the back seat. My
parents told me to calm down and hang up. They called my
sister and her husband who lived three blocks away and told
them to rush right over.

By then, my shift was practically done, so Maggie gave me
the rest of the night off. All the excitement was over anyway.
The crowd had gone home. My brother-in-law bravely started
up the engine, and my sister and I followed him to the farm,
watching the headlights and taillights blink on and off in response to little eruptions of sparks in the smoldering wiring.

The way I remember it, my parents were sleeping when
we got home, but that can't be possible. They must have
stayed awake to look at the car; we must have talked about it.
But my next memory of the event is that I woke up in the
morning, with my mother sitting at my bedside watching
me sleep.

She looked at me sympathetically as soon as I opened my
eyes. She stroked my hair and asked me if I felt all right. We
made small talk about my first night of work—had I liked it?
Did I get a lot of tips? I began to tell her I was sorry about
the car, that I had no idea.

"I know," she said, "some hoodlum must have come by
and thrown a cigarette in the backseat as a prank."

"Uh-huh," I said, biting my tongue. "It must have been
some hoodlum."

I don't know why my mother granted me amnesty that
morning—some act of kindness that I'll never be able to re-
pay. But the secret weighed on me. I wanted to tell it as I

watched my mother and father get the wiring repaired in the car, and as they made phone call after phone call to salvage yards trying to find a blue front and back seat to replace the burned seats.

They were only able to get a blue front seat. The back seat, the rest of the time we owned the car, was green. And the smell was awful—that sickly sweet smell that always follows fire. It refused to be aired out of the car's upholstery. My father found a body shop in Bismarck that said they could eliminate the smell by filling the interior of the car for three days with a pink foam that was guaranteed to suck the fire smell from the car. The only problem was that the pink foam left a cotton candy smell in the car that was almost worse than the fire smell it had removed.

I wanted to tell them as we drove to church each Sunday. I wanted to tell them, sitting on the green backseat, I wanted to tell them, as the blue Chevy that smelled strongly like pink foam cotton candy rolled to Sunday Mass, I wanted to confess.

But I never did tell them, and they never asked. Because in my family, we gave each other a wide berth, we did not inquire further. There are some stories in a family that are just too embarrassing for everyone to hear. A few months later, my father traded the car away and bought another blue car— this time a Ford.

Hard to believe, over thirty years ago now, the night that I drove into the moraine to park with my first lover, a man much older than I, before he was my lover. I remember how we lay in the back seat of his '56 Chevy and panted for each other, two bodies that burned to be one unbroken skin. How to describe, so many years later, the ripeness of my body on that night, the soft, white flame of want?

So young and too soon, we go out into the world after nights like this thinking it will always be this way—that our blood will always burn for someone—not understanding how desire collects hurts and gripes, cautions and misgivings, how it is tempered, numbed, and peeled away in degrees.

After this, the initial loss, we wander through the world and look for signs of the familiar in the faces of those we meet. We get more outrageous and bold, more inventive and self-destructive in our search for it; we meet fellow travelers along the way, also in search of it. Of everyone we encounter, we ask, "Are you my lover, are you my lover, are you?" But it seems we have all forgotten the face of the beloved. He would be unrecognizable to us, even if we passed him on the street.

That night in the moraine with my first lover who was not yet my first lover, as we lay panting for each other in the back seat of his '56 Chevy, I will stop his hands, move my mouth away from his hot breath, and I will say something only a teenage virgin would say, something like "I thought you loved me even without sex," or "I can't, I can't, I can't do this." And I will force him to slip on his pants, pull on his shirt.

He will move into the front seat, disgusted, and quietly suck a cigarette down to a thin wedge of cinders, and I will join him, dressed now, my limbs shaky with the cold and with desire.

Angry in his frustration, he will crank the ignition hard, his hands heavy with yearning, and something strange will happen—a part of his motor, something small and metallic and whirring will zing up and shoot out of his engine, leaving two tiny punctures like hot bullet holes in the hood of his car.

We will both get out of the car and run our amazed fingers over the still-warm holes on the hood. We will turn around in the black night and feel our aloneness in that silent, watching place, until he agrees to walk the miles across the fields of the moraine to the nearest farmhouse where my father will be waiting up.

And although it will be a personal catastrophe for me, my father will have no choice but to fire up his high-powered tractor and remove the wreck of my not-yet-lover's car from our hallowed land.

These are all things that happened. These are things that happened to me in that strange, ancient place.

6

ON LOST AND CRAZY SISTERS

My grandma Geist had a crazy sister. Her name was Emma. She never married or had children, and she lived in California, a place that sounded wildly exotic to me as a kid growing up in North Dakota. Everyone in California, I assumed, had ocean views in their backyards and fruit trees growing in their front yards.

When we were shoveling out of six-foot snowdrifts at twenty degrees below zero, I imagined Emma in that California life, sitting on her sunny verandah in silk pajamas and bedroom slippers with marabou froufrous on top, eating hand-picked peaches slathered in cream as she watched the ocean swirl and wisp.

I use the word *crazy* because that's the term I heard growing up—either that or *verrückt,* a word the old folks used when they lapsed into German to keep important things from us. My friend who knows the language says that *verrückt* means spinning-your-finger-at-your-temple crazy, which I don't recall anyone doing. Only that they uttered the word with such emphasis when they spoke about Emma that it's one of the few words I retained out of all the streams of German I heard growing up.

In my grandmother's photos from her early years, Emma is the thin, blond one in the middle, with a stylish dress and shapely legs, looking as if she's about to make some fun for everyone. Her shy brunette sisters stand on either side of her, squinting at the camera through their wire-rim glasses. They look like wardens or safety officers in their flat shoes and cotton shifts.

How Emma went from being the fun, crazy one with wild ideas in her youth to the paranoid schizophrenic one who needed to be institutionalized in her old age, I don't know. I only recall that my grandmother received letters from her. I was too young to read, and she never offered to share their contents, but I often watched her read them at the dining room table. Sitting down with the latest stack of mail, my grandmother would study the swirls of her own name and address, scrawled on the front of the envelope in Emma's distinctive hand. Slowly she'd wind the stems of her wire glasses around the curve of her ears, then pick up the letter opener and slit the top of the envelope.

"What does it say?" I'd ask after a few moments of silence.

"Oh, nothing important," she'd answer absentmindedly, folding the letter's delicate sheets and slipping them back in the envelope.

Questioning my mother years later about these letters, I discovered they were full of paranoid accusations: "They're trying to kill me"; "They're trying to get all my money." But who *they* were was never made clear to anyone in our family. What so tortured my grandmother, I think, was that her younger sister was growing older and more insane every day and that she herself was too old, poor, and far away from California to help Emma. She'd remove her glasses and sit at the table, kneading the tired sockets of her eyes with her fingertips.

The silence in my grandmother's house during those times was disturbing. The only sound was the ticking of the clock and the ever-staring eyes of relatives who watched quietly from photographs on the dining room buffet.

In the center of that ocean of faces was a color portrait of Emma, professionally done with a smoky studio background and the photographer's signature embossed in gold on the bottom right-hand corner. It was an eight-by-ten-inch glossy, three times larger than anyone else's photo, which meant that the wedding and school snapshots of distant and minor cousins attached themselves to it, tucked into the swirling edges of its thick gold frame.

In the photo, Emma is caught in profile, her hair swept up in a French roll, her mouth slightly open, her head thrown back, as if the photographer has just captured her saying something extremely witty. She's wearing cat-eye glasses—absolutely cutting-edge fashion at the time—and a brocade dress that shows off her slim arms and bare shoulders.

I remember the photo in such detail because I stared at it often, trying to reconcile the Emma in the photos with the Emma about whom the old people whispered, *verrückt*.

These were the days I spent with my grandmother before I was old enough to go to school, and my mother had taken a job at a store in town to supplement our farm income.

At first my mother tried taking me to a babysitter, Mrs. Mueller, a German hausfrau type who in my childhood imaginings bore an eerie resemblance to the wicked crone in all the grim European fairy tales—the woman with the crooked nose and the thin, stooped shoulders who wants to enslave and eat little children.

But Mrs. Mueller was not mean. Mostly I remember her ever-present apron and her incessant baking of bread, which caused a constant dusting of flour to be on her clothes, hands, and face. Mrs. Mueller's house was gray stucco on the inside and the outside, with a trampled brown lawn, an out-house, and old rusting cars and broken-down sheds leaning in the backyard.

The Family Clothing, the store that my mother had started working in, was situated on the last block of Main Street. Mrs. Mueller's house was one block off of Main. Even then, I was looking to better things. I was no more than four, but I knew that my grandmother had just moved to town. Some-times we went to her house for Sunday dinners.

From my bearings, I suspected my grandmother's house was a block down from Mrs. Mueller's on Main Street, di-rectly across from the park. I had a vague memory of the slides and swings. One day, after my mother dropped me off at Mrs. Mueller's I went in search of my grandmother's white house with green awnings, her trimmed lawn, and her splashes of pink flowers.

It took me two separate tries to find the house, sneaking out of Mrs. Mueller's each morning, trotting down the alley, through the rows of garbage cans and the raspberry bushes, until I finally found my grandmother working in her garden. After that, my mother knew I was ruined for babysitters, and she never took me to Mrs. Mueller again.

This is how I came to spend so many hours alone with my grandparents in that house that contained no kid things, only grandma-and-grandpa things: a root cellar, a sausage tub, and a ringer washer in the basement; talcum powder, corn pads, and shoe stretchers in the bathroom; a grandfather clock that ticked and ticked through the silent afternoons; packs of old letters with rubber bands run around them in the closet; and lots of photographs.

Just as my grandmother's dining room buffet was a treasury of framed photos, so her house was a family matrix, the place where all the relatives eventually stopped when they visited our town. Her own mother had died young from an infection contracted during childbirth. She was buried somewhere near the family land, in a location that no one can easily recall. The sepia-toned portraits of my great-grandparents, Katherine and Frederick Hoffer, set in dark oval frames behind curved glass, watched over us from my grandmother's dining room wall.

My great-grandmother came to this country, as all of my mother's family did, from Lutheran villages in the Glueckstal region of New Russia, west of the Dniester River on the Black Sea. My great-grandfather, Frederick Hoffer, the man Katherine would marry, had immigrated to Dakota Territory in 1899 with his two brothers.

After the Hoffer brothers left Russia, their father died, leaving their mother a widow. So in 1902, Frederick arranged for his elderly mother, my great-great-grandmother, to come to America and live out her last years among her children. But she arrived with a new husband, a widower named Dockter from the villages. This Mr. Dockter brought with him his young daughter, named Katherine, the woman who would become Frederick's wife.

Although I'd like to believe it was mad love or instant attraction, it's more likely that it was just convenience or family pressure that prompted Katherine to marry Frederick—technically her stepbrother—later that year, a fact that makes me especially sad when I read that she died in 1920, from complications after delivering her eighth child.

In the only photo I have of my maternal great-grand-mother, she's standing with a pail in her hand beside a tarpaper shack wearing a long dress cinched tight at the waist and at the neck. Standing on the steps to her right, in order of the tallest to the shortest, are three of her small daughters in immaculate white dresses. A black Labrador, who's been dead for at least eighty years, stands in the foreground with his tail pointed.

What's stunning about the photo is Katherine's elegance—her upright posture and formal dress, set against the squalor of the house. On the edges of the photograph behind the shack, the treeless horizon of North Dakota stretches forever.

Katherine died a few years after the photo was taken, at forty—younger than I am as I write this—and I wonder if it is possible for me to find her, living as I do, in the next century with no children and too much education, writing these words to her and all the other lost women in my family who lived early in the last century with nothing but more work, more children, and the unrelenting horizon to face down every day.

My grandmother was only thirteen at the time of Katherine's death. The two older sisters, Mary and Anna, who were around fifteen and sixteen, quickly left home for marriages in other cities. This is a story that's repeated and repeated again if one asks questions about the early days in the territory—the family that fragments like an exploded star, at the loss of the mother. The oldest children take over the field work and the womanly chores, and the youngest children are farmed out in ones and twos to various relatives.

When they near adulthood, these children marry quickly or join the military, spreading out into the world and rarely looking back to the site of the original, painful disaster. Against this wave of destruction, my grandmother, only a teenager herself, imposed her will by pulling people to her. When she married at sixteen, she and my grandfather took over her father's land, which made them the keepers of the Hoffer homeplace.

It's a strange thing about people whose families are tied to the history of homesteading. Even if we don't return to the Midwest to see our families, we still feel this tie to the original homestead. It looms in our imaginations, no matter where we migrate to. We know the trees we watered as children and imagine them now to be fifty feet tall, never returning to discover they've withered and died or been chopped down long ago.

We know the location of the barn, the chicken coop, the roads that lead out, and the fences that hem everything in. We could walk this territory in the dark, it appears so often in our dreams. And the couple that now lives on the land, even if they are not blood relatives, become a kind of original couple to us, the people who keep the candle burning in the window every night, we imagine, to light our long way home.

In this way, my Grandma and Grandpa Geist became the locus for my grandmother's floating, angry, dislocated siblings. All her life, she tracked their progress. When I was a child, it was enough for me to point to a photograph and she would reel out the history of the person: who he or she married, where they lived, what their in-laws were like, how many children they had, diseases, divorces, career changes, accidents, lost limbs, military service, and any other upturns or down-turns of fortune they may have endured.

She had a tracking and cataloging instinct that drove her to keep a special photographic log of all the people she'd known who had died. In this album, she'd paste photos of the deceased in their caskets, horizontal with their hands crossed in that final bed of gathered satin, the pallor of death spread across their powdered skin and painted lips. Beside the photo she'd tape the memorial card from the funeral along with a copy of the obituary or any other newspaper articles about them.

She understood acutely the beginnings and endings of things, how closely they are connected, and she felt that fragility of life in every moment. She'd buried her two infant sons, both of whom died within their first year of life, so she held tight to my mother, her only living child. And when we were born she held onto us, her grandchildren, with her large encircling arms.

She had constant access to the full spectrum of emotion— the sparking wire of joy and its opposite, the bared and broken plunge into grief. I watched each day as she cauterized those two ends into a circle and inhabited the hot place where they were joined.

When you went to visit her, even if you'd just seen her the day before, even if you were just stopping by on an errand, she'd greet you with tears in her eyes as if you'd been off on a long journey. She'd raise her warm, wrinkled hands to your face and pull you to her, your foreheads meeting, and in that moment you could feel that place inside the circle that she kept clear for you, and there was nothing you could ever do to change that basic, natural fact.

Every family has a lost or crazy sister, someone who whether by choice or accident has become unmoored from the flow of the family. She's the woman, the slight mention of whose name is often followed by silence, the shaking of heads, the clicking of tongues. Her many changing addresses and the names of her many changing husbands are scarcely remembered and are recorded in light pencil strokes in the address books of the women in the family.

Her children, after she's brought them screaming into the world, fly from her, spinning off like small satellites into the orbits of other families. If she remains childless, she is the name in the family genealogy from which no line descends, a dead end, a cul-de-sac in the ongoing road map of a family.

If you've ever heard how they speak of her, you would never want to be her, the one who's *vergessen*, meaning either the one who forgets, or the one who is forgotten. The one who, in forgetting her place inside the circle, is forgotten.

"If you keep going like this," my mother used to say to me, "you're going to end up just like your Aunt Emma."

This was usually yelled up the stairs in the direction of my bedroom, where I would be deep inside my closet, one arm in, one arm out of the twentieth shirt I'd tried on that morning. For some reason when I was a teenager, it was impossible for me to go anywhere without first trying on every single item of clothing in my closet.

I'd pause, a turtleneck ringing my eyelids. In my mother's world, there was always an *if*, and there was always a *then*— her statements were like geometric proofs clicking off in deeply inevitable ways.

But listen to her cadences, "just like your Aunt Emma," five hard stresses followed by one unstressed syllable—the letup, the way out, if I am to heed her cautions. And listen to my mother's erasures—*your* Aunt Emma, not *my* Aunt Emma—as if through language she could rearrange the generations and unlink herself from the chain.

There is fear in the whispered inquiries about the lost and crazy one, as if merely speaking her name will activate some dormant code and draw her to you, through locked doors, down from attics, unlocking genetic formulas, striking you wild in the head.

Wildness, vanity, being too high-strung, or too full of yourself, these are signs that you are a child on course to becoming an extravagant adult. So you must be monitored at all times, admonished and harnessed by turns, and generally tempered. Every trip my mother and I made to Bismarck to buy school clothes ended in a scream fest (her) and a crying jag (me) as we tried to reach a compromise about what she would buy me to wear for school that year.

There was an alarming gulf, it seemed to me, between my aristocratic good taste and her peasant leanings. I dreaded going into those clothing stores in the mall full of track lighting and flattering skinny mirrors because I knew I would want the blouse made of natural fibers with the nice label and the big price tag, and she would always find something easy to wash in a sensible color on a sale rack.

She would pull my treasured object from the hanger and turn it inside out to examine its seams. In her immigrant-born, depression-bred way, she knew how to uncover the blouse's structural secrets to ascertain what kind of trouble it would cause us down the road.

I never considered the limitations of her resources, all the clothes she had to buy not only for herself and my father, but also for my three older sisters and my brother. All I understood was my own want—surely an earmark of the lost and crazy one.

Deep on the top shelf of her closet, stashed behind her purses and shoe boxes, she kept coffee cans full of silver dollars she'd collected over the years from her part-time job in town. For years whenever customers paid her with a silver dollar, she would exchange it in the till for her own paper dollar then bring the heavy coin home to the coffee can. Here was the silver cache that would save us when the next depression hit.

Is it surprising that as a teenager I smuggled many of those silver dollars out of her closet and took them to town, where I exchanged them for cigarettes, French fries, and multiple pinball games?

I liked the way those coins filled my palm, their solid weight, and I loved the satisfaction of spending them—the translation of the saved thing into a fluid, living experience. I can still see myself as a teenager, a skinny punk in the Rec Hall, slamming and rocking the pinball machine, a cigarette resting sideways on the glass so the ashes would fall to the floor, or leaning back with a pool cue in one hand and a cigarette in the other, inhaling and exhaling my mother's nest egg into smoke.

How my fiscally conservative mother came to be the beneficiary of Aunt Emma's extravagance is not clear to me, but I do recall one day when we were all teenagers that a box came in the mail for my mother from California, full of Emma's hand-me-downs.

Inside were spiked heels in Easter egg colors and veiled hats, fancy lined dresses and tailored jackets. But the one piece I remember best was a sleeveless sheath made of a caramel-colored bouclé with filaments of gold running through the weave. When you undid the long hidden zipper in the back, you could see the dress had a gold lining, and a lush label with the designer's name scripted at a chic angle.

I can still see my mother spinning like a fashion model in the middle of the living room for us girls, the dress hugging her svelte figure, which was trim, not from dieting but from hard work. The dress hung just as elegantly on a hanger in her closet for years, untouched, along with the unused accessories—a sleek gold clutch with a fancy clasp, the slim, gold leather belt, and the gold, pointy-toed, three-inch spikes. We girls might have dared to try it on when mother wasn't around, but it seemed to emit a humming, glowing force field that kept it pristine in its isolated corner of my mother's closet.

How might my mother have worn such an outfit in our small town, where the slightest difference in dress or manner marked you as *unter Acht und Bann,* an outsider, the one who does not belong? And now I wonder how my mother disposed of the dress. It wasn't as if she could have included it one year with all the other hand-me-downs at the church rummage sale. It was too beautiful to rip apart, and it wasn't made of the right material to be used for rags.

It would be hilarious to find a three-inch square of it in one of my grandmother's quilts, woven in with all the other three-inch squares of cloth from my third-grade Easter dress and all the other handmade dresses worn by my sisters as we were growing up. These quilts were like family history lessons, mosaics with one overarching theme of rigorous sameness.

Finding swatches of Emma's caramel-colored bouclé dress woven into one of my grandmother's quilts would be as fantastic as imagining Emma herself stepping out of a limousine on our small Main Street, Bacall-like, in dark sunglasses and asking the driver in a husky voice to please bring along her steamer trunks.

To some, the fact that Emma sent the fancy dresses to my mother testified to the fact that she was fully bats-in-the-belfry insane or completely unaware of how unlike us she had become. Either way, she was too far out of our circle to be reclaimed; she was lost to us.

She left North Dakota in the hard, brown days of the 1930s, and she never returned. The photographs that came from California were full of sunny streets with Emma posing in front of downtown storefronts with her arms thrown around another handsome soldier. There was never a husband in the pictures, just lots of different men whose last names my grandmother never knew, and whose first names she did not bother to scribble on the back of the photo.

Emma was the sort of woman about whom people would say, even years later, that she had been a real beauty. As she aged, she remained thin and stylish, even as my grandmother became shorter and rounder, her face and arms taking on a doughy softness. Only in the end, after Emma's mastectomy and the six-year fight with cancer, after the institutionalization and the electroshock therapy, did she lose her luster, her beauty falling away from her as did her mind. But by then, we were no longer receiving letters or pictures.

My friend who is a sculptor tells me the practice of crazing in ceramics involves exposing a clay sculpture to extremes of temperature by putting it through the firing and cooling phases too quickly. The result is that the thin, outside glaze contracts at a different rate than the larger, stable clay body underneath, and the result is an intricate weblike pattern of hairline fractures that appear on the surface.

The effect in a clay pot is beautiful, a kind of distressed perfection. But what about such surface fractures when they appear in a person? People who knew Emma as a young woman described her as nervous, high-strung, particular, and "not quite right," indicating a youthful sensitivity. It causes me to wonder if an already fragile mind, when exposed to severe shocks and extremes, is more vulnerable to crazing.

As a child, I had superstitious ideas about what had caused Emma's mental illness. Could California, that wild place, have driven her insane? My father used to say that long ago the continent was tipped on its side, and whatever wasn't nailed down ended up in California. Poor Emma had ended up in California with all the other flotsam and jetsam.

Her younger brother Adolph, my grandmother's living brother, writes me a letter in answer to my questions about Emma. Of course, it was a long time ago, he explains, his hand shaky and illegible. But he vaguely remembers that Emma survived a boating accident on the Sacramento River in which both her fiancé and her best friend drowned.

What must it be like to be orphaned of your mother at ten, to fight your way out of rurality and poverty into paradise, where you attract new friends and someone who loves you, only to lose everything again in one afternoon?

"That river," Adolph writes, "I don't know why they went near it. Every year someone drowned in that spot, and still the people keep going."

But even this makes sense to me. Of course, Emma would go to that river, find the location of the most swirling, dangerous currents again and again. We are all drawn to that deep, down-turning place that wants to pull us under. But without her mother or another woman to tell her the story about what happens to the little girl who goes too close to the cliff, the little girl who wanders too far into the forest, the little girl who doesn't know to look for the wolf's whiskers under the grandmother's sleep bonnet, what chance would any of us have of surviving?

The Jungian psychotherapist Naomi Ruth Lowinsky wrote about the motherline—that feminine lineage, the successive generations of women in a family who believe in you well before you exist and remember you long after you are gone. A rupture in the motherline, Lowinsky observed, has serious ramifications, which include the loss of family knowledge, stories, recipes, culture, and a sense of one's place in the family line. Without the strong feminine presence to tack us to our family, Lowinsky wrote, we might "wander like motherless children in the too bright light of masculine consciousness."

I see Emma in those words as I read them, just as I see myself, the young woman growing up in the 1970s, so anxious to leave home, so eager to unstring myself from the line of women in my family, their foolish cautions and stern reprimands, so hungry for reinvention.

I see myself in Emma's vanity and extravagance, a woman who uses her body for fashion and recreation, for her own pleasure and the pleasure of men who are not good for her, men she barely knows.

"Where are my grandmothers?" Virginia Woolf cried for her lost literary foremothers, their ancient texts buried deep and unrecovered. I grieve for my grandmothers who died too soon, or died without talking about such things, or died unheard because I wasn't listening.

I think most of my two great-grandmothers who died in childbirth as I stand at this precipice—in my forties and without children, terrified my whole life of taking my body into that dark cave of childbearing, from which I've seen women emerge either rich with child or broken beyond repair, but emerge nevertheless forever altered.

The survivor-woman in me who knows how to find food, make herself useful, attract mates, and win fistfights, the hunted girl who is quick with her hands and feet, good at being a moving target, impossible to hit, has never dared to enter that dark cave of making.

"There's a moment in childbirth when no amount of breathing helps," the poet Norita Dittberner-Jax wrote, "when you finally understand that you are the subject of your own life, and your situation is serious." I think of my grandmother, Lydia Geist, delivering all three of her children in that small bedroom on the farmstead in central North Dakota where her own mother died young, and where so many things went wrong. What kind of strength does it require to go to that bed each night, sleep, make love, and try to bear more children?

My mother tells and doesn't tell the story of what happened to her two lost brothers. She infers and sighs, tells it in fragments as if I already know the full shape of the story no one has told me.

"They should have gone for the doctor," she says, "but you know how poor they were." The first baby boy died of influenza two months after being born. A few years later, the next boy was born, his arm and collarbone broken, his eyes blackened from the brutality of extraction. He died the next day.

No one ever talked about how my grandmother managed to rise up from that bed where she must have been broken as severely as her child. How did she bind together the torn and bloody parts of herself without a doctor and assume the care of her one living child, my mother, who was four at the time. No one ever talks about how Grandma Geist went back to her farm work, milking cows and shocking grain into tall sheaves.

There are many stories of women who did not rise from these beds, but hers is not one of them. She who saw no importance in her own story. She who lives inside us now like a shimmering web, catching us, keeping us right.

7

BETWEEN EARTH AND SKY

As I get older, I become infinitely interested in everything older than I am—old people, old letters, photographs, and papers, ship manifests, yellowed newspapers, crispy deeds, buried archives. For years, no trip home to see my parents seemed complete without a visit to an older cousin's house to ask questions about the old days, or to an old folks' home, or to an abandoned cemetery.

On Memorial Day, 1994, while visiting my parents, I went with my mother to place flowers on the family graves. My mother pointed out the double plot that she and my father had recently purchased. It surprised me that they had chosen a spot toward the center of the graveyard, close to the fifteen-foot statue of Jesus hanging on the cross. All the other family graves are located in the front row facing the highway. Driving into town, one can see my surname repeated on the tall head-stones—Marquart, Marquart, Marquart, Marquart.

"We thought it would be nicer in this spot," my mother said, pointing out the plot's proximity to the suffering Jesus. She was on her hands and knees, weeding crabgrass from what would someday be her own grave.

"Visit us." She turned and looked up.

Vertigo overtook me, the sound of water rushing through my eardrums. "Excuse me?" I said, afraid to hear it again.

"After we're gone," she said, returning to her weeding. "Don't forget to visit us."

When we got back to the house, I asked my father about Great-Grandma Marquart. I hadn't seen her name among the headstones.

She's buried, my father explained, near Hague, a town sixty miles south, near the place where my great-grandfather originally took up a land claim when he arrived in the United States. After great-grandmother died, he remarried a widow, another immigrant from the villages, and moved both families north to Napoleon, buying the farm our family now owns. So Great-Grandpa Marquart is buried here with his second wife.

That night, I asked my father to show me where the first Great-Grandma is buried, and we agreed to head out early the next day. I suddenly felt sad for her, buried somewhere south of there, alone in a land that must never have ceased to be strange and unfamiliar to her. It seemed important that someone from my generation know where to find her, although I'm not sure what would compel such a need.

I've often wondered why Great-Grandpa sold off his original land claim in McIntosh County and bought the larger property where I grew up in Logan County. Was the land so much better? Were the memories of my great-grandmother too acutely tied to the original homestead for him to bear staying there? Impossible to know—people didn't talk about such things back then, and anyone he may have confided in would be long dead.

The house that Great-Grandpa built on the original homestead in McIntosh County is still there, my father told me. It's ensconced inside several additions and renovations, but two of the original outer walls can still be seen. My father wanted to show me the site and, if possible, he wanted to introduce me to the family that bought the land from my great-grandfather in 1900.

We almost didn't get out of the house the next morning because my mother discovered that sector C, the southwestern quadrant of her sprinkler system, was not functioning. Although we only planned to be gone for about six hours, my mother didn't like the idea of leaving home when anything was out of kilter.

It was only 7 A.M., but already she had called the repairman who lives two blocks away in our ten-block town. He promised to come and fix it, but she really wanted to be there when he arrived. Then my father started fiddling with the master controls, the dials and the timer clock housed in the garage, which made it even more certain that we wouldn't get out the door that day.

As my parents got older, I tried to make it home at least twice a year to visit, usually at Christmas and sometime during the summer. Teaching at a university two states away made it even harder for me to keep up with their interests, which seemed to dwindle in number but occupied increasingly larger amounts of their time and energy.

When he was alive, my father insisted on going to the post office by 8:05 A.M., to pick up the mail the moment it hit the box, or the day would be ruined. My mother continues to hold a part-time job cleaning the church. The town that felt so small to me growing up seemed to shrink even more as my parents aged.

My life, conversely, branched out to new places, spreading farther and wider. As it did so, it grew more abstract and difficult for my parents to comprehend. They could so little imagine the quality of my days, who my friends were, how I made my living, that they would have trouble formulating the first question. Before I called them, I'd try to turn myself back into the person they remembered as their daughter.

There's a story that goes around in my family that my paternal great-grandmother, Barbara Hulm Marquart, upon seeing the strip of land in central North Dakota that she had traveled from south Russia by boat, rail, then oxen to claim in 1885, fell to the ground and cried, "It's all earth and sky."

I'm told it sounded better in German—*Das ist ja alles Himmel und Erde*—and I don't doubt it. Growing up as a grandchild of immigrants in a small town populated largely by ethnic Germans who had fled Russia, I was constantly reminded that everything sounded more clever or grave, more funny or profound, when uttered in the mother tongue.

Perhaps my grandmother responded to the treeless, unbroken plain of grassland in much the same way as did Beret, the Norwegian pioneer woman in Ole Rölvaag's classic novel of immigrant experience, *Giants in the Earth:* "All along the way, coming out, she had noticed this strange thing: the stillness had grown deeper, the silence more depressing." She realized it had been weeks since she'd heard a bird sing.

In *Giants in the Earth,* Beret grew to pathologically fear the expanse of the plains. She described it as a "bluish, green infinity" in which there was no place to hide. When another pioneer caravan passed through and pressed deeper into the unimaginable void, Beret watched the settlers' wagons as they grew small on the horizon and disappeared under the brow of heaven. "But whether into the earth or into the sky," she thought, "no one could tell."

What Beret must have sensed was missing in that expanse of green and blue, and what my great-grandmother may have instinctively feared, was that missing sliver, a small margin of culture necessary in the landscape for survival—not a culture of opera or ballet, but a culture of potatoes and onions, pots and pans, doilies, curtains, and bed linens, in which children could be fed and sheltered.

And into that negative space, my great-grandmother must have known, she would be expected to pour her days and nights, the work of her hands, and all of her imagination to bring shape to these things.

On the journey across the country, my great-grandmother was pregnant, as was the character Beret in *Giants in the Earth.* On the wagon as they approached their land, Beret's husband, Per Hansa, thought about his wife's condition: "Beret was going to have a baby again. Only a blessing, of course—but what a lot of their time it would take up just now! Oh well, she would have to bear the brunt of it herself, as the woman usually did."

I remember these lines even though I read the novel almost twenty years ago. I find them easily because they are underlined. And I understand as I read them again that I have been looking for my grandmothers for a long time, searching deep in the crevices of old maps and books for them.

Genealogies are never enough. How sad to think of a whole life reduced to these dry facts—birth and death, marriage dates, the inadequate words *Wife* or *Mother* chiseled on a tombstone in a graveyard no one knows to visit.

My great-grandmother Marquart did not last long in America. She died in childbirth in February 1900, fifteen years after her arrival, attempting to deliver her eleventh child, a daughter who would die with her on that day.

I have nothing tangible with which to gauge the quality of her life—no photographs, no worn-thin wedding bands, no engraved silver platters—only this single line she is known to have uttered at perhaps the most desperate moment of her life.

I learned the barest bones of her story from my father's first cousin Tony who remembered better the older generation. His father died in the influenza epidemic of 1918, within a week of Tony's birth, so he was taken back into my great-grandfather's house and raised there. He remembers his grandparents as vividly as most children would remember their parents.

On an earlier visit home from my teaching job, I called up Tony and asked him if I could stop by and ask some questions about the older generation. Soon I found myself sitting at the round oak table in Tony's big kitchen, listening to him talk about Great-Grandma and Great-Grandpa. My father came along to ask his own questions and to hear Tony's answers.

Both men were in their seventies, but they looked remarkably young, as the men in my family tend to. They were both short with very slight builds, and their facial features, like mine, when viewed from certain angles looked slightly Asiatic. But what I noticed most as I sat listening to Tony is how much our hands were alike—small hands with a long, narrow palm and a well-shaped thumb—although Tony was missing a joint on his left middle finger from what, I assumed, was most likely a farm accident.

And what struck me even more that day was how much our gestures were alike. As we talked, we all placed our hands on the table in front of us, fingers clasped together in the shape of a pyramid.

Most of my adult life, I have lived out in the world in cities and university towns with men and women from every conceivable part of the world, so the sight of so many small hands shaped like my own on the table before me was stunning. For that moment, I saw my hands as part of an ongoing chain of hands—no longer mine, free to do whatever they pleased, but bound to my ancestors by blood, mannerism, and duty. As the only writer in my family, and the first generation to attend college, I checked my palms and thought, *These are the hands I was given to write with. Now what is there for me to do with them?*

My great-grandmother, Barbara Hulm Marquart, did not leave Russia by choice, I know that now. She left Kandel, her village on the steppes near the Black Sea, to follow my great-grandfather Joseph who was on the run from forced induction into the Russian army.

Historically, German-Russians were a gentle people whose abilities blossomed in the presence of plants and animals. Over the centuries, they sought fertile, low-lying plains for their farming—the lush Rhine valley of central Europe in the 1700s, the rolling steppes of south Russia in the 1800s. Unfortunately, these farmland plains were also ideal terrain to roll troops across. So we are the people whose crops have been trampled by every major despot and emperor who has tried to make a land grab on the continent of Europe.

We Russo-Germans will never mold history; history will always roll violently over us. In old war novels and movies, look for us. We are the anonymous dead nobodies left to rot in the countryside, our pockets turned out, our shoes stolen, our faces bloodied to an unrecognizable pulp while the hero destined for history books marches on to the capital city.

For this reason, I find myself empathizing with the powerless at every turn. I scan the crowds of refugees on CNN, looking for faces that resemble those of my great-grandparents. Watching episodes of *Star Trek,* I grow anxious for the new crew member, the one who is not part of the permanent cast, when he is enlisted to join the Away team. I know he will be the one to catch the incurable virus or be vaporized on Planet X, 10 million light-years away from home.

In the same way I have always felt sorry for Antigonus, the loyal but shortsighted lord in Shakespeare's *The Winter's Tale*. Faithful to a fault, Antigonus delivers the baby girl-child Perdita to the wild, stormy hillside where her father, the king, intends for her to perish. And with this loyal act, Antigonus terminates his usefulness to the plot.

In fact, the story so requires that Antigonus not be alive to reveal the secret of how he disposed of Perdita (so the surprise is maximized later in the play when she appears, fully grown) that the only thing for the playwright to do is kill him. Shakespeare disposed of him in the most economical way—"Antigonus: Exit, pursued by bear." The sight of that infamous stage direction saddens me. Reading this, I decide never to be useful to kings, never to hold their terrible secrets.

Guns have never fit well in our hands, so molded to the scythe and the plow. To avoid a fight we have several times picked up and moved to another continent. But every few generations, some of us are born angry or stubborn, or perhaps as foolish as the miniature toy poodle I once observed who was so yappy and bold that he barred me from passing him on a sidewalk. He didn't understand that even though he was barking with big-poodle genes, in reality he was only a palm-sized dog.

By all accounts, my great-grandfather, Joseph Marquart, was such a person, a small man with big plans and lordly ambitions. Like Per Hansa in Rölvaag's *Giants in the Earth*, he looked out on the unbroken grassland while his wife collapsed in tears beside him and thought to himself, "I am going to do something remarkable out here, which should become known far and wide. This kingdom is going to be *mine*."

For years it seemed, I found my great-grandfather in every third novel I read. In Jane Smiley's *A Thousand Acres,* he's the land-hungry father, Larry Cook. In Willa Cather's *O Pioneers!* he's the land-loving settler John Bergson, who even from the grave would have appreciated the look of a full field of grain, "so heavy that it bends toward the blade and cuts like velvet."

In William Faulkner's *Absalom, Absalom!* I found my great-grandfather in the character Thomas Sutpen, a stranger who appears in Yoknapatawpha County with a mysterious past, whose goal it is to possess one hundred square miles of land and produce a solid lineage of children flowing out of him into the future.

I found a reflection of myself in *Absalom, Absalom!* as the young, preoccupied Quentin Compson, "listening, having to listen, to one of the ghosts . . . telling him about old ghost-times." His very body was an "empty hall echoing with sonorous defeated names." Quentin was not a being, Faulkner wrote, he was a "commonwealth."

My own constituency includes multiple layers of grand-mothers buried in unmarked graves and complicated totems of grandfathers resting heavy on my shoulders, all of them waving subtle whiffs of stories before me then telling me to construct the rest out of the fragments.

On the morning of our proposed trip to Great-Grandma Marquart's grave, after the repairman arrived and the sprin-kler once again demonstrated its proficiency in sector C, we were off, heading south to the site of the original homestead of my great-grandfather.

On the road, driving south of Napoleon on Highway 3, my parents were quiet in the car. They had turned on a country western music station, and my father tapped his fingers on the wheel to the beat. My mother hummed lightly. They both watched the landscape go by, pointing things out, making elliptical comments that I couldn't decipher from the back seat.

My parents were consummate observers of the landscape. What were the hundreds of things they knew about this place that I could not see—drainage patterns, the knowledge of crops that would thrive here, signs of erosion, names of wildflowers, grasses, and trees?

Driving south, we passed through the moraine of rocky hills left by the last glacier. Tucked inside the ridges and slopes were farms—clusters of houses, barns, outbuildings, grain silos, cattle grazing in green fields, farm equipment parked at random angles in grassy yards, cultivated farmland spreading out for miles. Many of my friends from high school grew up on these farms. As we passed each one, my parents updated me on recent history—which son took over the farm, who he married, what became of the rest of the kids.

After a long alienation from that place, I wanted to see it again as my parents did, as a variegated, complex thing, a place to spend one's whole life studying and loving. For many years, I felt an aversion from home, an overpowering flight impulse upon which I believed my very survival depended.

But now I can recall blissful days of early childhood on that land. In fourth grade, we were given an assignment to identify trees by collecting their leaves and classifying them. After school that day, I remember walking the long rows of the orchard that bordered our farm, on the hunt for leaves.

Our family always called this five-row band of trees the Orchard even though, aside from chokecherries, it never contained fruit-bearing trees. It was a tree belt, frankly, a wind shelter for the farm. Great-Grandpa must have called it the Orchard, an indicator of the grandiosity of his dreams for us, and perhaps some trace memory of the estates that he recalled from his childhood in Russia.

Now I can recall my rapture on that warm, fall afternoon walking through the protected rows, the cloistered quiet, the sound of birds, the light breeze, the sun coming through the branches and touching my face in strobes of light.

I must have completed the school assignment; I have a vague memory of pressing the leaves into a small book with a cool iron and wax paper. But that day is the last memory I have of being unequivocally happy in the natural world. After that, all my associations with the land are of hard work, the incessant wind, chores, lifting, sweating, feeling exposed in weather that was too hot or too cold.

Very soon, I retreated into the antiseptic world of books. My attentions migrated to the more pleasant things of the world—music, television, fashion. I was hijacked by popular culture. But now as I approach my fifties and live hundreds of miles away, I want nothing more than to find once again that blissful place on family land, wandering happily through rows of trees on a sunny fall afternoon.

We found my great-grandmother's cemetery easily enough. Inside the lace of iron in tall letters was the name of the now defunct church—St. Andrew's Parish. The old church was boarded up, but the graveyard was well maintained. The summer had been warm and dry, so the grass was bristly under my sandals. We passed through the gate that opened under an ominous wrought iron archway.

Her grave was marked with an iron cross, a tradition among German-Russians. In the early days of settlement, the blacksmith served a dual role in the village—one pragmatic, the other artistic. He was called on to build an iron cross grave marker out of spare shafts and curlicues of iron. These iron crosses, which are sprinkled in Catholic German-Russian graveyards throughout the Dakotas are now historically preserved, so we found that my great-grandmother's grave marker had been painted with silver paint to protect it from deterioration.

I stood with my parents in the warm sun and looked down at the name on the small plate—Barbara Marquart, 1861–1900. I milled around the graveyard with my parents. Having found her and visited her, we didn't know what else to do.

If a trip to an abandoned cemetery was not sobering enough, near my great-grandmother's grave on the edge of St. Andrew's Parish cemetery we found an even more devastating sight—a row of identical iron crosses, seven in total.

When we studied the name plates, we learned the reason for their uniformity. Six of the names were of children, all with the same surname, who had died within days of each other. Within one week in 1918, it appeared from looking at the vintages, this family had lost six children ranging in ages from twelve to two. The grave on the end, the seventh, was that of an older woman in her thirties with the same family name, who died one year later, in 1919. Was she the mother who died of grief within a year after losing her children? It's hard not to construct a narrative around such a sight.

My father bent down and ran his fingertips across the letters on the steel plates marking the grave. "It must have been the flu epidemic," he said. Even though it happened a few years before he was born, he found it hard to believe that he didn't know the story. The row of graves indicates a scope of tragedy that usually carries a story that people for miles around would remember and talk about for years to come: "Oh, yes, that was the Schmidt family. All wiped out in 1918."

How do dramatic stories get lost in families? About my grandparents' passage to America, my father could not tell me even the smallest detail. From my cousin Tony, I learned the skeleton of the story. When my great-grandfather was a young man in Kandel, he was of the first generation of German colonists to be drafted into the Russian military.

I don't know how my great-grandfather was inducted, although I have heard stories from other families of Russian military convoys arriving in the villages late at night, going door to door, and demanding from each household one young man to serve. I have heard of women hiding their sons in the rafters, knowing that young men rarely returned whole if they returned at all. And I have also heard of those Russian soldiers stepping into the houses and firing their weapons through the roofs of houses to discourage the practice of hiding sons in rafters.

I do not know in which wars, if any, my great-grandfather fought—or if he could shoot a weapon, or if he ever killed a man. It's only from his obituary that I learned he rose somehow to the rank of officer.

But Tony remembered Great-Grandpa telling the story of how he was smuggled out of south Russia—*in der Dunkelheit* is the phrase Tony says Great-Grandpa always used, "under cover of darkness." I asked Tony what could have caused him to run away, to risk leaving behind his family, his wife and children, all his property, all the people of his village.

Around the slim remnants of this story, there were, no doubt, many heart-pounding moments of terror and exhilaration, but these have all dropped away over the last 120 years. The short answer, the only known detail that remains, is that one day my great-grandfather flew into a rage and struck a commanding officer—a *Feldmarschall,* as Tony recalled the title, a Russian field marshal.

What could have possessed my great-grandfather to lose all concern for self-preservation and strike a powerful Russian superior? This act is not consistent with what I know about my meek and evasive ancestors. With this detail I must come to terms with either how principled and irrepressible he was, or how foolish and impulsive he may have been. Did a court-martial or the firing squad await him at daybreak?

My great-grandfather survived his act of insubordination with the help of a fellow officer, also a German. The German superior must have been powerful to accomplish the things that I know from the family story happened next: My great-grandfather was smuggled that night out of the country and eventually made his way to Bremen, Germany, where he spent several months waiting for my great-grandmother and their children to follow.

I try to imagine my great-grandfather riding away from the night sounds of a soldiers' camp somewhere in the middle of Russia in 1885. He moves silently as if floating on an invisible river, and as he rides the sound of the army diminishes, becomes softer and softer until all he can hear is the sound of his horse, the clopping of hooves on the dark path.

So nice for him—a farmer by inclination and trade—to be back in the presence of pure nature. Perhaps he carries a sack with a few small potatoes in it, a pinch of salt. Does he stop by the side of the road to eat and draw some water from a stream? Maybe he has a companion to help him across the border; maybe he is alone.

He sits down by the creek and listens to the wind moving through the trees, feels the cool grass beneath him. He is tired and a bit stunned by the events that have transpired in the last twenty-four hours. He thinks of his wife, my great-grandmother, and of his three small children back in the village on the Dniester River just north of the Black Sea. Will he ever see them again? Will he see his mother and father, the church where he was married, the school where he taught before he was drafted? Before him in the long night are only unknowns and a silence that stretches out into the darkness.

For this moment I want to think of my great-grandfather as simply a young man, as uncertain of his future as I am in my own life each day. He is sitting in the dark by a creek, eating stale bread, on the run from the Russian military. For this moment, he is simply a traveler—out of all place and time. None of the assurance of the photographs he will take later in life in America is with him now.

When we look at our ancestors in pictures, it's easy to think of them as people whose lives are settled, written, complete. We imagine they lived in simpler times, but behind those sober, unsmiling faces, behind those formal black clothes, one can be certain there was great suffering—a woman's pinched mouth betrays a lifetime of anger against her husband; a child's hunched shoulders indicate he's itchy and uncomfortable in new clothes; a husband's confused expression reveals that he wonders why his wife produces all these daughters and so few sons.

In that dark night, does my great-grandfather tear off a piece of bread, try to calm himself by eating it? He is twenty-nine years old. Beside him on the ground is a small, olive-colored wool blanket he will sleep on for the night. Close to him in the dark, chewing and snuffling, is the horse he will ride to the border.

He realizes he has just committed the most brilliant or the most stupid act of his life, and right now he has no idea which it is. The only thing to do is lay his head down on the blanket, feel his heart beat, listen to the stream move in the darkness, and know that he is as alone, helpless, and as untethered in the world as he has ever been.

The ground beneath his sleeping head is some of the most well-traveled and consistently inhabited land in the world, the great Pontic Steppe, which throughout time has been the contact zone for groups as diverse as the Kurgan people; the Scythians, who traveled in nomadic packs across the steppes from Siberia; and the Sarmartians, another nomadic Indo-Iranian group.

According to Neal Ascherson's cultural and natural history, *Black Sea,* the land where my great-grandfather lays his head on this quiet night in 1885 has been home to a succession of settlers—"Tatar villages, colonies of Russian veteran soldiers and their descendants, Polish exiles, neat farming districts where almost everyone was German, Cossack *stanitsas*, and Jewish shtetls." Before that, this was home to Greeks, Thracians, the Prussians, Armenians, and the Moldovans, all in their own time.

West of here, near the Dniester *liman*—the widening of the river that flows by the village where my great-grandmother sleeps peacefully for this one last night—is the ruins of the ancient colony of Tyras, surrounded by the huge Turkish fortress of Akerman, now partially buried by the waters of the encroaching Black Sea.

This is the place in Russia my ancestors dared to call home. How did the German colonists come to believe—a mere seventy-five years into their inhabitation of these villages—that they belonged so completely to the steppe? In retrospect, it makes them seem naive, but I understand their feeling of surety.

When I was a child growing up in North Dakota, with only seventy-five years of family land ownership to inform and assure me, I could not imagine a time when my hometown, Napoleon, would not be there. Both of my grandfathers had been born in Russia; both of my grandmothers in America. We had old roots in one country, and new roots in another. What caused me to believe that someone of my blood would always live on our land? Yet I never doubted it. There is a comfort in that knowledge, the effects of which cannot be easily described or assessed.

"Never let the land go out of the family." This is a caution I heard often and always growing up. As the owners of the center farm, the original homestead, my family has been the caretaker of a legacy that's important, if only conceptually, to cousins and uncles and aunts who live in places far and wide.

On the day of my father's funeral this was the one thing that my brother heard again and again: "Don't sell the land." Our adult cousins shook my brother's hand and clapped his shoulder: "If it ever comes down to it; let me know, so I can buy it." These were dentists and teachers, insurance salesmen and owners of construction firms who lived three states away. These were people who had never spent one day on the land that is our family farm; still the land represented terra firma to them, some deeper sense of home.

What makes a piece of land go solid under your feet? How to explain this nostalgia for land that overtakes otherwise pragmatic people? Mircea Eliade wrote, in *The Myth of the*

Eternal Return, that "archaic man saw settled land as sacred and the wilderness as profane." Wilderness or uncultivated regions were part of the undifferentiated void, something to be shaped and molded to our needs.

When our ancestors performed rites of cultivation such as plowing, seeding, and finally inhabiting a piece of land, they saw themselves as "cosmicizing" it, making it sacred by matching its shape to the cosmic model. According to Eliade, people who settled virgin land felt themselves to be performing an act of creation. Like God, they were doing elemental things—separating the light from the dark, the land from the ocean. They were making order from chaos.

At that moment, no matter how difficult the work, they felt their lives take on a greater resonance. Their actions connected them to ancient, ongoing patterns—what Eliade described as a "ceaseless repetition of gestures"—and they felt their connection to a chain of being that stretched back beyond known ancestors. Family land, by association, becomes a symbolic locus, a geographical record of those sacrifices and successes.

From the few words I have to remember my great-grandmother by—"It's all earth and sky"—I can't say whether she lived long enough to feel that sense of belonging or accomplishment. Maybe she knew the place would destroy her.

In *Giants in the Earth,* Rölvaag's character Per Hansa observes about his wife Beret, "She has never felt at home here in America. There are some people, I know now, who never should emigrate, because, you see, they can't take pleasure in that which is to come—they simply can't see it!"

My great-grandmother's trip with three small children from Odessa, Russia, to Bremen, Germany, by rail, then to America by boat, then pregnant across the country to Dakota Territory by train, and finally to her homestead by oxen must have felt like some weird regression. It was as if she were traveling back in time, a reversal and undoing of her own grandparents' trek from the Rhine Valley east along the Danube River to Russia in 1803. She saw that they were starting over in the wilderness again. She missed her neat house, the fenced-in yard back in the village, the vineyards, the church, and all the graveyards where her grandparents were buried.

When the European settlers arrived in North America, Richard Manning wrote in *Grassland,* they discovered not the New Testament God of hedged-in villages back in Europe, not the "god of logic derived from thirty centuries of civilization." Instead, they encountered the God of Job, Manning wrote, "the god of fire and plague, a brutal and capricious creator like the predecessor god of the Christians, the Old Testament deity that had not yet consented to grace."

Is this what drove my great-grandmother to fall to the ground that first day on her new land claim—the realization that she had come face to face with the god-of-no-promises to whom she must prostrate herself? Perhaps this is why Willa Cather noted in *O Pioneers!* that "the Bible seemed truer here."

And what did my great-grandfather see in the vast emptiness as he stood beside her? By all accounts, he saw only promise and open space. It was almost as if he could reach his hands up and pull down heaven.

"America, Land of Opportunity," he had read these words on the broadside posters back in Europe. They were hung on the walls of stores by the railroad companies to lure immigrants to the American West. And now he could see for himself that the posters hadn't lied. In a few months, with the work of his hands, everything would materialize before him—he could see it all now—the endless fields of wheat waving like spun gold in the wind.

8

GREAT FALLS

Strange things happen to me in Montana. Starting with 1976, when my fiancé tried to convince me to move there with him for a job. This was before Montana became The Last Best Place, back when it was still The Assignment in Siberia. My single goal in life had been to keep myself east of the hundredth meridian.

He was just a crazy boy in crazy love with me, I understand that now, these almost thirty years later. Just as I realize now that I loved him crazy back. He was tall and self-conscious about his height, with thin hunched shoulders and a lean run-ner's body from the hours of training for the track team. There was a lightness about him. He had a deep voice and an easy laugh, and his hair was shoulder length and streaked gold from the sun.

We met in world religions class, at junior college, where I was starting just as he was finishing. When he left Bismarck for a track scholarship in another part of the state, I dropped out of classes, hitchhiked across the state, and transferred to a university in his college town, all in one day.

A few years later, with him, just twenty, and me, almost nineteen, we were mad to be graduated and together in married love. Weren't we just asking for it?

Those fevered winter sleeps in his Tenth Street apartment in Fargo, our bodies hip point to hip point, turning in the night. My shoulders lining the crook of his arm, his leg thrown over mine, light, even in sleep. My chin resting in the hollow of his collarbone, that sweet press of comfort, the comfort of enclosure.

And weren't we asking for it that spring weekend when we drove back to visit his parents in Bismarck, two hundred miles from our college town, and he took me up that steep ridge near the edge of the city one night and showed me the wide swath of land his wealthy father owned, all of it under development, although there were no streets yet, or signs of excavation, or gutters, or empty paved cul-de-sacs.

He stopped the car and had me get out. The headlights shone over this dark expanse, all as-yet undifferentiated land. And he pointed out where we would someday live. Our lot would be the choicest spot on the edge, he said, with the good view overlooking the lights of the city.

He paced it off for me in the flickering light, the perimeter of the house—where the kitchen would be; here, the living room; there, the bedrooms—his long arms making wide drawing motions in the air. He stood beside me and shaped his hands into a frame before my eyes, as if blocking scenes for a film he was directing.

I recall smiling at him in the darkness and nodding my head as he spoke, but some panicked part of me was thinking, *Wait, did we talk about this? Where we would live after we were married, what city, what state?*

And I thought I foresaw, in one bright flash, what would be my future life: a fat-faced baby banging a spoon in a high chair; strained carrots on the linoleum; a sky-blue telephone on the wall, ringing incessantly; his mother, my mother, always on the other end of the line wanting, I don't know, to exchange recipes.

For a moment, I thought I remembered I wanted to be something—a social worker, a rock star, a revolutionary—I wasn't sure which.

Here are the ways we lose each other. As soon as we get home, small things go wrong. His father, who owns an empire of businesses sprinkled throughout the West, begins to act like he owns much more. I begin to realize the boy I love receives paychecks each month, unearned, drawn from his father's business. *Rich boy,* I begin to think.

To make things up to me, he goes out and spends an entire month's pay on a diamond-opal necklace, my birthstone, and matching opal earrings. He shopped for them for hours—he tells me that night at the restaurant—going from jeweler to jeweler looking for the right fiery flashes of green to match the precious gems of my eyes. But all I can do is be angry when he doesn't have enough money to pay for dinner, and I'm left to pick up the check.

Wasn't he just a crazy boy who would blow all his money on presents and drive himself off a cliff for me? Ten dollars, twenty dollars, one hundred dollars, I think about it now—the stupid things we put between ourselves and those we love.

Because he came from a soft world, I suppose he didn't know that I could be such a hard girl. Because I was too young, I still harbored a belief that I was invulnerable to any breakage in the world.

Weeks later, he tells me we won't be moving to Bismarck after all. His father is grooming him for a job managing one of his businesses in Polson.

"Polson?" I say, afraid to know where we will be sent.

"Montana," he says, "on the southern tip of Flathead Lake."

"Montana." I begin to hyperventilate. It sounds as if he's drawn the short straw.

Things move quickly after that. Within months we are breaking up and broken up, and I am sleeping with a tall, willowy sprinter from Virginia, just so the crazy boy will understand it's over.

He married a girl with long, brown hair someone said, and they moved, after all, not to Montana, but to Bismarck where he started work in his father's empire.

And the house he imagined that night overlooking the city was never built. The couple bought a house, I found out years later, in his parents' subdivision, two doors down from the house where he grew up. And when I heard that small news item, I must admit, I thought to myself, *Man, I really dodged a bullet there.*

I have a friend, a traveling salesman, who swears his car breaks down every time he passes Eloy, Arizona, a small town between

Phoenix and Tucson, on the way to Nogales. Now, each time he gets near Eloy, he's tempted to take a detour, but he tells himself it's pure nonsense, superstition.

Then just as he passes Casa Grande, the engine skips or the tires begin to thump, the muffler rumbles and sparks begin to drag on the freeway, or a hose breaks, spewing antifreeze all over the windshield. It's true, he's an unreliable narrator of his own stories. And there's no way to check the truth of it. He does drive junkers, which increases the likelihood he'll break down anywhere, including Eloy. Still, I want to believe him. Because I know there are places that have memory, that harbor grudges and throw hexes. There are places in the world that have hard-ons only for you, and Montana is such a place for me.

The truly strange things that happened to me in Montana began after I dropped out of college in 1977, eight credits shy of a degree in social work, right after I broke up with the crazy boy who loved me.

For the next few years, I moved through bands—country western, then a wedding dance band, then rock, then progressive hard rock, then a heavy metal band. With music, it's just like what they used to say about drugs—you're always working toward the harder stuff.

By my fifth or sixth band, my soprano voice had gone deep and raw from stage screaming, and I was dressing now entirely in black. My hair color and my stage name had been changed, not to protect the innocent, but to protect some idea I had about who I wanted to become.

It was the early eighties, and I was living in Rapid City playing with a heavy metal band—a power trio of bass, guitar, and drums, with me up front singing and playing a little keyboard. We toured the West and sometimes Canada in a large black truck outfitted with couches and cots for resting as we drove, and a large bearing wall in the back half of the truck that held all of our gear in place.

The truly strange events that came to pass in Great Falls actually began several weeks earlier, the night before we left Rapid City for a two-month tour. I lost my driver's license that night, mysteriously it seemed to me, when I was stopped by a cop for a burned-out tail light in my Plymouth Fury.

That was the last I saw of my driver's license, my only form of identification, and I really didn't think twice about it—ever having to *prove* my identity—until three weeks into the tour when we had a sudden cancellation, a double booking in a club we were supposed to play, and our manager called to tell us he'd found a replacement gig in Canada.

It was easy to find last-minute work across the border in the 1980s. Canadians loved American bands, but no one wanted to chance the inspection. With a van full of longhairs and a truck full of equipment, the border guards thrilled at giving their drug-sniffing dogs a run through all your possessions.

We'd always gotten through, but you'd hear horror stories of speakers being ripped from cabinets and left on the side of the road, of guitars and sound boards dismantled, and of the

inevitable discovery of that lone pot seed nestled in the carpet. You might be there for hours, or years.

We had been playing in Bozeman, finishing up our week
at the Cat's Paw, when the call came about the gig in Calgary.
The pay was twelve hundred dollars for the week, which was
good money then, even though six of us had to split it, after
the 15 percent came off the top for our manager, and, really, it
was only twelve hundred in Canadian currency. We sat in the
motel room and weighed our options, which were few. We
were going to Calgary.

This is the moment when I had to introduce my unique
problem—my lack of identification—and all around the
room, I saw shoulders go limp, jaws go slack.

"How could you leave home without an ID?" our light
man scolded.

I was new to this band, only four months. The male singer
I'd replaced had a high, airy voice, almost feminine. The band
had made two albums with him singing all the songs in that
high voice, until he got married and his new wife said, "Uh,
uh, buddy, that's all the road life for you." So that's when they
came to Fargo looking for me. Because I was in between
bands, and my voice was high enough to hit their previous
singer's highest high notes.

The last three weeks on tour hadn't been going well. I was
losing my voice from all the hard singing, and, for the last few
months, I'd been messing around with my guitar player, who
was unhappily married to his high school sweetheart, a good
woman, now a civil engineer, who was happy to support him

financially, as well as cook, clip coupons, and clean house just to support his genius.

The guitar player had black hair, long and straight down the small of his back. He had obsidian eyes, dark dashes of eyebrows, and a heavy black mustache that was so long that he could, if he wanted, twist it up on the ends, handlebar style like those villains in Saturday morning cartoons.

He was troubled and brilliant—a classical pianist and classical guitarist—in addition to his heavy metal playing, which was hard and fast and gritty. He harbored a romantic notion of himself, I knew, as Attila reincarnated.

When I first joined the band, I would watch him tuning his guitars in his dark corner of the stage, hunched over in some cloud of constantly brooding blackness. Here was someone to test my mettle against. The indestructible girl in me perked up.

The real Montana trouble had begun earlier that week in Bozeman. I was taking a bath one night after the gig to wash the sweat and salt from my skin. The guitar player was sitting on the edge of the tub as I bathed. We were discussing the night's performance, what songs had gone well, what needed work. And this is the moment that I chose to give him an ultimatum—the next time we returned to Rapid City, I said in a calm voice, he would either have to leave his wife or give me up.

He shot to his feet and began to shout. I rose in the bath water and stepped out of the tub naked, somehow knowing it was better to get away from the water. I reached for a towel just as he grabbed me and began to shake me, his thumbs pressing into my arms.

My first response was shock. No one had ever touched me this way. My father was an exceedingly gentle man with an explosive temper that he reserved only for the weather and farm equipment.

It was slippery on the tiles and cold, with my dripping hair, my wet skin and feet. I struggled in his grasp, and that's when the first slaps came, hard on my face, which so surprised me that I began to scream and flail my arms, which only made him pin me tighter against the wall and slap me harder.

He was strong, I realized then, so much stronger than I, even as I fumed and bucked against him with my thighs and knees. After some time, after I had no strength left, when I finally went limp, he released his grasp and we sank to the floor together, both of us crying now. And then a long silence followed.

People always speak with impatience about women who stay with violent men, wondering how they could be so stupid. But people don't realize that many violent men, as violent as they are, are equally gentle afterward. They are so sorry, sorry, sorry. And each time, they manage to convince you it was an anomaly, that it will never happen again.

We spent the rest of the night in bed. He, on his knees beside me, crying, begging forgiveness, touching my swollen face, the scrapes on my shoulders, the thumbprint bruises on my arms, saying over and over that he couldn't believe what he had done.

We didn't sleep. We waited for the sun to come up, and we watched the bruises develop around my left eye and cheek, light blue and pink in patches, and eventually, by morning, a ripe purple half-moon rose under my left eye.

I met the band in sunglasses the next morning, making small excuses. The band didn't ask questions. We played out the week like that, with me fronting the band. I sang more ferociously under the harsh stage lights, my bruises covered by the wide rims of dark shades.

Road musicians are notorious problem solvers. A few days before we were to leave for Canada, after I'd revealed my lack of proper identification, the guys came up with a solution— all I needed was a certified copy of my birth certificate.

But I couldn't call my parents. The arguments I'd had with them over the years about dropping out of college, about bands and breaking up with fiancés and having no money, had left them so disturbed that we had reached an impasse. When I had joined this band, one state away, four months earlier, I couldn't bear to tell my parents. I couldn't afford to hear the disappointed sigh on the other end of the line, so I had just packed up and moved to Rapid.

Disappearing was easy. I couldn't even be sure they had noticed me gone yet, but I liked to imagine their wild concern when they finally called and found my old number disconnected. How can I explain the wicked pleasure I took imagining their suffering? *They'll be happy to see me when they find me,* I remember thinking, *or they'll be sorry when they find me dead.* Who was this person—so young and sadistic, and eager to dash herself against the rocks?

So to retrieve my birth certificate I had to call my old fiancé, the crazy boy who once loved me. There was no other choice. He now lived in Bismarck, the city of my birth, the location of the state capitol, and the permanent home of my birth certificate.

I swallowed hard and dialed the number. It struck me then as amazing that all one needs is the exact arrangement of seven digits to dial straight into someone's life. The casual hello of his wife's voice on the phone sounded strange and far away. She didn't ask who was calling.

He came to the phone in a few moments; I could hear him moving through the rooms toward the receiver, the sound of the television in the background, and then his voice was on the line, still warm and deep and friendly. I explained my situation. Could he go to the state capitol in the morning and retrieve a certified copy of my birth certificate? I asked if he could seal it in an envelope and put it on the Monday morning westbound Greyhound bus, which would arrive in Great Falls, by our estimation, around the time that we were passing through that city on our way to the northern Montana border crossing in Sweetwater.

How many years had it been since we'd spoken—three or four? Yet he agreed easily. It was nothing, he said, a small thing to do for an old friend.

Great Falls, despite its lofty name, does not boast great falls. A stony ridge marks the cutbank of the Missouri as it meanders through the city. On the north side of town, some outcroppings reveal a series of shallow shelves that drop and make their way to the turbines of the Rainbow Dam. This is the part of the Missouri that gave Lewis and Clark fits when they tried to portage it, but that was two hundred years ago in birchbark canoes.

We came upon Great Falls in the late afternoon, just as the light was fading. We found the Greyhound bus depot on the crustiest street on the edge of the small downtown. We parked our big black van outside the bus depot and waited for the westbound, which was due in by nine. We laid back and settled in. It was October and the days were getting shorter and cooler.

Our soundman estimated that we could be to the border by midnight. With no delays at customs, we could be to Calgary by morning, just in time to sleep, set up, and play the next night. I felt relieved. Great Falls would be a stopover.

In the end, we spent two days parked outside that Greyhound bus depot, our truck moving up and down the street in increments to avoid getting a parking ticket. Every two hours, our soundman would rouse and crank the engine, pulling a car-length forward to the next parking spot, all the time singing, "Lovely Rita, Meter Maid," as he did so.

Westbound buses came and went, at the rate of two or three a day. The people behind the Greyhound counter came to know all of us, shaking their heads, *No,* each time we approached looking for my birth certificate after the latest bus.

The westbound buses stopped in Great Falls for short layovers, taking on passengers, then plunged further westward in the night, toward Spokane, toward Seattle. We lived and slept in the van those two days, taking turns dozing on the couches and cots. We used the depot facilities, brushing our teeth, washing our faces in the bathrooms. Strangers came and went, mounting and dismounting buses, lugging their crying children and heavy suitcases.

I spent much of those two days in the phone booth just inside the front door of the bus depot, dialing and redialing the work number and the home number of my former fiancé. Sometime on the first night, he had stopped answering his home phone. Imagine? The next morning, his secretary claimed not to know how to reach him, although I left message after message.

Between dialing, I'd retreat to the bus depot bathroom and take off my sunglasses to study the migration of blue bruises on my face. Then I'd return to the phone booth, pull the black accordion door closed beside me, pick up the receiver and dial again. *This would have been my home phone number,* I thought as I dialed. *If I hadn't been so stupid, this would have been my phone ringing in my kitchen.*

The days stretched on endlessly. The band took walks, bought giant cookies, got coffee, visited a porn shop down the street, talked to the drunks who congregated and begged for change outside the door of our van. One guy actually said to me, "I'm a quarter away from a gin and tonic," as if he were endeavoring toward some noble goal, like raising funds for better programming on public television.

With each westbound that came and went without my identification papers aboard, the guys in the band grew more frosty and impatient. By now, I was hiding in the highest of the back bunks. I was crying, holding a pillow over my stomach and my hand over my mouth so no one could hear my sobs. At one point, I overheard the light man in the front seat, saying, "All I know is, ever since *she* showed up bad things have been happening."

When the guitar player finally found me hiding in the back bunk and saw that I was crying, he asked me what was wrong, and I blubbered, "I miss my cat," which made everyone roll their eyes. Who was this stupid girl, and could we just leave her by the side of the road?

She's so many selves away from me, these twenty-five years later, she's barely recognizable. But I must claim her, that black-haired girl dressed in black, with a black eye hidden under dark sunglasses. I feel the tug of recognition whenever I dare to think of her. If she is one small bead on the necklace of myself, then the self I am now, even though dozens of beads away, is still strung together with her on the same unbroken thread.

My birth certificate arrived on our third night of waiting. On the evening of the second day, we had pooled all of our money (we had eighty dollars between us), and we rented one motel room so we could all take showers. Each day that passed we were losing portions of that twelve hundred in Canadian currency, but our manager assured us that Calgary still wanted us, no matter how many days late we arrived.

When I finally reached the crazy boy on the phone, the morning of the third day, he acted casual, as if he were popping his forehead over his forgetfulness. All apologies, he promised to put the envelope on an airplane that very afternoon. We removed ourselves from the Greyhound bus depot to the airport parking lot, waiting out the afternoon until the flight landed.

The plane was three hours late that night, due to engine problems, but I can still see our jubilant soundman running across the dark airport parking lot toward the van, waving the manila envelope that held my birth certificate over his head as if it were the Holy Grail.

He got in the van, tossed the envelope to me in the back, grabbed the key and fired the ignition. Sweet freedom. We were peeling out of the lot and headed for the border before I could even rip open the seal.

I'd like to say that something significant changed in me the night that I was handed my birth certificate. In the dome light of the van, I read it with fascination—my father's name, my mother's name, the date, place, and time of my birth—as if I were a double agent memorizing the details of my new identity.

But the person I was at birth seemed as unrecognizable to me at twenty as my twenty-year-old self seems strange and inaccessible to me in my forties.

A few years ago, while on other business in Montana, I rented a car and took an afternoon drive north to Great Falls. If you live long enough, it seems, you have time to revisit the sites of your most spectacular disasters.

I arrived to find the windows of the bus depot soaped over and boarded up. The depot, someone told me, had long ago been moved to the airport. The neon signs for the dive bars were torn down; the porn shop was closed, as was the giant cookie store. All the drunks were long gone or dead or dried out. I stood on the street for a long time, incredulous, as if I'd been stood up for a much-anticipated date. This street had been going on, business as usual, in my imagination all these twenty-five years.

I tried to peer in the soapy windows, but it wasn't even possible to glimpse a sliver of the objects I remembered inside—the curved oak waiting room benches; the wooden phone booth with the hard black seat; the silver slot of the telephone into which I had pumped dime after dime; the scuffed door to the bathroom with the smoky glass window that read, "Womens." It was a cold November day. I drove north of town, to the banks of the Missouri and sat in my car watching the water cascade down the shallow falls.

I spent the rest of the afternoon in an antiquarian bookstore in the center of town. When I began to quiz the owner about the history of the region, he asked me what had brought me to Great Falls. I told him that I was a writer and that I was researching the worst three days of my life that I'd spent there twenty-five years before.

A woman, overhearing, nosed into the conversation. "A writer," she said with disgust. "Well, don't write anything bad about us." By then, Montanans had had enough experience with writers to believe what Joan Didion has said about them: "Writers are always selling someone out."

I don't wish to write untruthfully about anyone, but is it possible to speak precisely through memory? That self-destructive girl with the black eye works best as a fiction, like one of those cigarette-smoking characters in an existential novel whose motivations, though fascinating, we will never fully comprehend.

My understanding of her comes in small flashes, but there's never a cohesive whole, no unifying theory. And memory works that way, too, in flashes. We create the illusion of fluidity by supplying the connections.

I have one lasting image of her standing in the bus depot bathroom, studying herself in the mirror. The lighting is low-wattage, almost browned out, and the reflection is stretched and distorted, because in the bathroom, instead of glass mirrors, they have installed unbreakable sheets of silver plastic that offer a carnival's house-of-horrors reflection.

She has taken off her sunglasses, and she's leaning over the sink to get a good look at the progress of her bruises, the purple half moon still ringing her left eye, the lighter ones on her cheek beginning to fade.

Then I remember she does something strange—she leans directly into her garbled reflection and says out loud, "Who are you?" No response. Only the echo of her voice against porcelain.

"Who are you?" she asks again, as if questioning a prisoner whose name she will want to document in a report to the authorities.

Who is she? Stupid youth, unbridled appetite. She's a woman who doesn't believe the laws of the universe apply to her—not the passage of time, the force of gravity, or the curvature of the earth. Whatever is troubling her cannot be loved away or beaten out or screamed clean.

One day, the crazy burning girl in her will simply lose speed and altitude. She will fall heavily to the ground and break apart, extinguished in her own flames. One day, she'll crash and burn, giving all of us a much needed rest.

9

TO KILL A DEER

Later, everyone would agree it was the least likely time to be encountering a deer. The two young guys in baseball caps who stopped to help me and my parents on the freeway said it, as did the highway patrolman who arrived in his cruiser to fill out the report after the two guys in baseball caps went to the next town to call for help.

Even the old man who arrived with the truck to tow my parents' wrecked car seemed perplexed. He removed his greasy cap and scratched his head, as did the manager of the body shop to which our car was eventually towed. Everyone agreed that a deer should not have been on that stretch of highway at that time of day during that time of year.

Montana was movie-beautiful that morning in 1995. We'd left Bozeman before dawn, full of the coffee and pancakes my sister's husband had risen early to make for us. I took the wheel in the semidarkness. My mother got in beside me, and my father took the back. We were glad to be heading home, done with the three-day visit. I imagined the sun barely kissing off the flat eastern horizon of North Dakota—the place where I hoped to deliver my parents safely home by nightfall.

The Yellowstone River snaked beneath us, crossing and crisscrossing under the freeway, as if to escort us out of the state. At every mile marker a view presented itself like a tourism postcard begging to be snapped. Montana was green and gorgeous that day. It was strutting around, ready for its close-up, and we were sick of it.

We sped east out of the mountains, into the sunrise, reaching Livingston as the light began to fill in the horizon. We drove through the passes, flanked on either side by the giants of the road—the Gallatin Range spreading long and wide to the south, the huge blueness of the Big Belt Mountains to the north, and in the distance the craggy top of Crazy Peak.

My father was sitting in the backseat holding the nitroglycerin pill under his tongue that would quiet his racing heart. He had spent his life working the unspectacular farmlands of central North Dakota that looked as if they'd been laid out with a carpenter's level. Something about the mountains always made him short of breath.

I was in the driver's seat with my right arm slung casually over the wheel trying to assume that confident-driver pose I'd seen my brother Nick take on so naturally whenever he drove a car. I hummed lightly under my breath and spoke when spoken to, and then only in forced monosyllables, just as Nick would have done if he'd been there. I stared straight ahead and drove, only taking my eyes off the road long enough to watch my father struggle for breath in the rearview mirror.

This was the fourth trip I'd made to Montana with my parents, so I knew that his condition would correct itself when the dramatic elevations leveled out to the mundane flatness of the central plains. Then he would lean back in the soft upholstery of the Oldsmobile. "At last, God's Country," he'd say, in a voice ringing with disgust over being lured away from the quiet splendor of North Dakota.

In his old age he remained forever uninterested in places like Florida, Hawaii, and other fabulous retirement spots. In December on my Christmas break, or in August on my summer break, the last thing I wanted to do was get on the road and head north, north, and ever northward into fierce blizzards or sweltering heat.

"For once," I've begged, "can't someone I'm related to live in a temperate climate?"

After retiring from farming, my father kept himself enormously busy with small but critical tasks—mid-morning coffee with the other retired farmers, who would sit at café tables in their clean overalls, chew on toothpicks, and talk about the crops. That done, my father would toodle out to the family acreage in his pickup to see how many farming mistakes my brother Nick might be making.

It was only when we, his moved-away daughters, shamed him with news of our various children, weddings, graduations, and anniversaries that he was forced to visit us in the neighboring states we'd flown to. Once away from home, he was determined not to be impressed by anything he saw.

About Mount Rushmore he might have said, "So it's a bunch of faces in a rock. We've got plenty of rocks at home." He could dismiss the entire continent of Europe with a wave of his hand—"Ah, everything is so *old* there." About the Grand Canyon, he would have said, "We drove two thousand miles to see a big hole in the ground?"

Every spring for several years we made this trip into the Rockies to Bozeman to visit my oldest sister Kate. My parents were the tourists; I was the daughter-driver, the accommodating travel guide. It was a concession I made in my forties, to compensate for the wild rebellion of my teens, the mad raging of my twenties, and the sullen intractability of my thirties. Every spring when the school year drew to a close and my desk was scattered with unfinished drafts of poems, revisions of stories, and portfolios to grade, I received the first Montana inquiry.

"Of course, we could drive ourselves," my mother would say to my answering machine in a polite voice. And soon after that I'd call back and find a date in my crammed calendar. The last day of school, I'd turn in my final grades, and get on the road, driving the first 750-mile leg of the trip by myself from Iowa to North Dakota. From there, we'd take my parents' car and head west into big sky. The first year we made the trip, my very nice husband went along, but later he knew all of us a lot better and couldn't be convinced to do that again.

Once on the road, I submitted myself to my parents' whims and routines—start out before sunup, mandatory pie stops in the late afternoon, pee breaks allowed only at locations preapproved by my mother. At first it seemed strange to hear my old name, Debbie, which no one has considered call-ing me for twenty years. But I didn't try to correct them. My mother still referred to me as "the baby" when she intro-duced me to people, a habit I was never able to break her of no matter how nasty and unbabylike I became. So I minded my own business and drove the car, drinking in as much of the sagebrush and rolling foothills as I could without putting us in the ditch.

Every year, no matter how I prepared myself, I was surprised by the first sight of mountains. As a born and bred flatlander, I seem destined to be forever in awe of mountains. In much of eastern North Dakota, where the horizon is especially flat, the only hills we have are the off-ramps the Feds created when they built the freeway. Once in the mountains, I tried to convince my father of the beauty of the place.

"Look there, Dad," I'd say, pointing to the nearest eight-thousand-foot peak. "See how that one just pierces the clouds?"

He'd scan the horizon, his nose turned up at the very no-tion that *this* could be big sky country ("You wanna see big sky? I'll show you big sky."). My mother caught on and filled in the silence with small enthusiasms, things like, "Isn't that something," or "Gee, I never noticed that before."

After some time, my father would raise his hand and point his knobby finger at the mountain, not at the peak, but to a small level clearing at the base of the mountain.

"I see they got in a few acres of wheat there," he'd say. This is the farmer's view of the world: If you can't plow it or seed it, what the hell good is it? "What a waste" was his most-repeated phrase from the backseat.

My mother was in the passenger seat folding and refolding the maps. This is something she would do until we got home. But what's to check? We've all made this trip several times, and from Bozeman to Bismarck it's a straight shot: I–90 to I–94, then we're home. Two hundred years ago, Lewis and Clark found the way without much trouble.

Still she felt compelled to give us updates: Livingston, 100; Billings, 175. By her calculations, we would make lunch in Miles City by noon exactly. She loved the symmetry of this and reminded us repeatedly that Miles City was the exact halfway point between Bozeman and home.

I knew that when we arrived at Miles City we would eat at the same truck stop where we'd lunched every time we made this trip. I no longer took issue with this. One year when I suggested that we try the 4B's family restaurant on the other side of the overpass, my mother was thrown into such a frenzy that I'd never mentioned it again.

My mother is trim and perky, with a smooth, rounded curl-and-comb hairstyle. Her life is driven by the twin purposes of precision and economy. As a child of the Depression, she was raised to despise waste of any kind. She goes to bed late, gets up early, keeps a spotless house, and wrenches as much as she can out of each day. "I like to make things with my hands," she will say, showing off the row of cabbages she's grown, the batch of cookies she's baked, the cotton blazer she's sewn.

As her most extravagant and accidental daughter, I have not registered very often on my mother's Richter scale of achievement. With a failed career as a rock musician (where I squandered my twenties), a bad first marriage to a brooding guitar player, too much college (where I wasted my thirties), and no children to recommend me, I have gone so far into the red with her that everything I do meets with suspicion. Even in my forties, I doubted that my career as a writer and a teacher would salvage me in her eyes.

Both she and my father were full of nervous inquiries about my work. For example, whether I was "on break" or "unemployed" during the summer when I was not teaching was something my parents often quizzed me about. When I made the point that the summer is a good time for me to catch up on my research, they remained unconvinced. How could I do research without a laboratory? This seemed like fuzzy logic to them.

When I tried to explain that my writing *was* my research, it came out sounding like one of those nebulous excuses you concoct as a teenager when you're asked to account for a missing block of time: "Yeah, the library. That's right, I was at the library." They worried and wondered, how could I possibly have that much to write about?

They were equally perplexed by my teaching load. Once, when I called home to tell them I'd been hired for a tenure-track position and now would only have to teach two classes a semester, my father got silent for a time and then nervously asked, "Are you able to get in a forty-hour week, then?"

When I explained that with my "research" I worked well over a forty-hour week, he was still unsatisfied. Thinking I had gotten myself into another hopeless situation, he suggested that maybe I should call up my new employer, Iowa State University, and ask if they'd let me teach a few more classes.

Here I'm reminded of a story Jay Leno told on the *Tonight Show* about his mother. After he replaced Johnny Carson on late night, he was anxious to impress his mother with the lucrative deal he'd just signed. Trying to give her an idea of the elite millionaire's club he'd just joined, he bragged to his mother about some of the actors he'd be rubbing shoulders with, people like Sylvester Stallone and Bruce Willis.

Why, just that week, Leno boasted, Arnold Schwarzenegger was coming on the show to promote his latest film. Then Leno made a point of mentioning that Arnold's contract for his latest role was upwards of $23 million.

"I guess that's not bad pay," Leno said, "for three months' work."

"Yes," his mother conceded, "but what does he do for work the *other* nine months of the year?"

Take away most of the zeros, and this is how incomprehensible my career path was to my parents. Tenure tracks, sabbaticals, Fulbrights ("If you get it, will they force you to leave the country?")—hopefully my parents would remain blissfully unaware of all the dead ends and potholes on that road. I returned to the policy of my youth—the less they knew about my life, the better.

Still it was lonely out there in the world without them. That spring I was buoyed by the release of my first book of poetry—something solid to show for all my troubles—and by a piece of family gossip I'd received from Elizabeth, my second oldest sister, in Minnesota, who believed my status in the family had been upgraded from Outcast to Rebel.

Elizabeth went back to school in her late thirties to get a degree in nursing. During her training in an ER, an ICU, and a psychiatric hospital, she managed to find diagnoses for all of us. In our family we now had attention-deficit disorders, chronic thyroid problems, and congenital heart conditions where we once had only vague paranoid feelings that something about us was terribly wrong.

Some of us, my sister was convinced, were borderline obsessive-compulsive. I considered this diagnosis as I watched my mother page endlessly through the little black book she kept with her when she traveled. In this journal, she had jotted down vital details about all the stretches of highway she had ever driven.

High on her list of things to note in her little black book were gas prices, good food stops, cleanliness of rest rooms, and easy access on and off the freeway. In it she had sketched rough aerial perspectives of the on- and off-ramps she had taken. An engineer from the DOT couldn't have done a finer job.

She meant to avoid any of those roads that veered wildly to the north and never returned you to the freeway, or those off-ramps that cloverleaf into endless circles, causing you to lose your bearings. One false turn and we could have ended up in Canada or Wyoming or some bad neighborhood in Los Angeles where we would be mugged, carjacked, and never be allowed to return to North Dakota again.

Watching her pore over the drawings and scribbled notes in her black book, I was reminded of my own book of published scribbles, *Everything's a Verb.* All during this trip, I'd waited for some indication that my parents had read my book of poems. Two months earlier, I had signed a copy, packed it into a padded envelope, and held my breath as I dropped it into the mail slot. That was the last I'd heard of it.

When I got to their house earlier in the week, I had looked around for it. Would it be displayed on the coffee table, or maybe nestled in the magazine rack along with mother's AARP newsletters and back issues of *Prevention* magazine, dog-eared from so much use? But it was nowhere in sight. I went in search of my book, eventually finding it in my mother's sewing room wedged on the shelf between the town centennial book and the Betty Crocker cookbook.

All week the silence about my book worried me. Had they found the nasty poem I had written about my mother—"I Am Upstairs, Trying to Be Quiet"—the one my friend, Julie, calls my "teenage-mother-hate poem"? It begins with the lines:

> *when i think of her, i think of silence,*
> *my mouth growing tight across my face*
> *after she has told me not to sing*
> *in the house*

The poem goes on to depict an emotionally killing relationship between a mother and a daughter. I still remember my palms sweating and the rush of adrenaline the night those words appeared, as if written by another hand, in the pages of my notebook.

In the poem, the girl has chronic dreams that the family home is stormed by street gangs, rock bands, and Nazis who "trash the furniture, raid the refrigerator" and "have their women in her bedroom." In the end, the girl hides "upstairs, trying to be quiet" while the intruders are downstairs, tearing the mother "limb from limb."

If my parents had read the poem, I wondered, would they ask me what it meant, and if the "I" in the poem was me, and if the "she" in the poem was my mother? And how would I answer them? Would I reel out a teacherly explanation, scolding them that it's all a metaphor, and that one should never assume the "I" in a poem is the author?

Before I shipped the book off to them, I considered cutting "I Am Upstairs, Trying to Be Quiet" from the collection with a razor blade, excising it so cleanly that its absence would not be noticed. But I quickly found that removing the offending poem meant that the second page of "Motorcade," my poem about the Kennedy assassination, would go with it, which meant that I would have to take the first page of "Motorcade," too, and then I'd have to eliminate the last half, then all of another poem, and so on and so on. In total I found I would need to extract nine pages from the book—a gap so flagrant in a slim volume of poetry that even my parents would have noticed.

My sister Elizabeth, who is also an artist, finally calmed my fears, assuring me that our parents would never read the book because they'd be "too grossed-out by the cover," which featured a surreal Peter Dean painting of three women emerging out of the water with their pink nipples glistening. Her predictions had proved accurate—so far, I'd heard no mention of the book, not on the twelve-hour drive to Montana, not during the two days at my sister's house in Bozeman.

Instead, my mother chattered about her cleaning job at the Catholic church. The monotony of travel, it seems, put all our mouths on an endless tape loop, like some Muzak version of small talk: We repeated to each other hourly the five or six things we knew for certain.

On the way home, my mother became fixated on the evergreens—the way they grew straight out the side of the mountain. She repeated this observation several times, and I agreed with her each time, answering with a light, "Uh-huh," all the while monitoring her voice for tone, waiting for that slight inflection that indicated she might veer off into anger or disapproval about the poems in my book.

"Two hours to Miles City," I whispered into my shirt-sleeve as we passed the industrial smoke stacks that mark the outskirts of Billings. By nightfall, I would have them safely home. To pass the time, I imagined my burgundy-colored van, with all its fluid levels topped off and ready to go, sitting in my parents' driveway, patiently anticipating my return so that I could hop in, turn the key, point its nose southeast and never look back.

It was ten in the morning. My eyes were already drowsy with sleep, but I refused to yield the wheel. I cracked the window open for fresh air and popped myself on the side of the head a few times to wake up.

My mother sat in the passenger seat with her white purse tucked neatly under her legs. She reached down every few minutes, I noticed, and touched it with her fingertips to make sure it was still there. Once we cleared Billings and the land started to level off, I pressed down hard on the accelerator, set the cruise to eighty, and pushed into the open road, letting the Oldsmobile swallow up miles.

I saw the deer a second before we were upon her, time enough to tap the brake and release the cruise, but not long enough to warn my passengers or slow the car. In a field to the right, sunlight reflected off a shallow creek. Perhaps she had sheltered there the night before in the small stand of trees winding along the water line.

She moved through the green, the grass thick and high around her, and then she stepped delicately through the opening and onto the pavement. There she hovered in the emergency lane with her tail end toward us.

She seemed to be taking in the day, the cool velvet of her nose sniffing out the crisp morning air. Later I would recall how she looked to her right first, to the open field where the creek flowed lightly over rocks; then she looked to her left, to the twin lanes of worn pavement. For a second, she twisted her neck to look behind her, staring down the road to where our car was screaming toward her.

Don't do it, I thought. She seemed to look straight at me. I gripped the wheel. I only needed her to stay inches outside the right lane. Her eyes were black and luminous and filled with a kind of dew. "Don't even think about it," I said.

She swayed to the right for a moment, to that endless rolling prairie that waited beyond the ditch, then she turned and stepped left into the driving lane, the tawny brown of her body growing large in the windshield, meeting with the powerful front bumper of the Oldsmobile. The hood crumpled up, pieces of fiberglass flying to the side, as we pushed through. Her body lifted up, then glanced off across the left lane, finally coming to land in the grassy median between the east- and westbound lanes.

A group of cars rushed by as we slowed, their tires crushing debris and scattering our chrome and fiberglass down the road and into the ditches. Feeling the front end wobble, I tapped the brakes and angled the car into the emergency lane.

My mother put her hand on the dashboard; my father sat forward in the backseat as we inched to a halt, the radiator already blowing a thin plume of steam. Everything in the car was silent for a moment.

My first thought was of my father. Would his heart survive this? I glanced at him in the rearview mirror. He was sitting up, breathing easily, more alert than I'd seen him in days. He caught my eyes in the corner of the mirror.

"Are you okay?" I said to his reflection. He nodded yes with a stunned expression, as if to say, "That was some ride."

"I didn't even see it coming," he said.

"I knew it," my mother said from the passenger seat in a wavering voice, her fists in her lap. "I knew we shouldn't have left home."

"Are you hurt, Violet?" my dad said to her, putting his hand on the front seat headrest.

"Oh," she moaned, "I just had a feeling something bad was going to happen." She rocked in her seat and clutched at her pant legs.

"Are you okay?" I repeated, studying her now. Physically, she appeared unhurt.

"My car," she began to cry, putting her face in her hands and rocking her shoulders. "My nice car."

"Oh, Mom," I said, thinking about all the other ways this accident might have turned out. "That can be fixed." I put the car in park and turned off the ignition.

"The most important thing," I reminded her, "is that we're all okay."

"But I bought this car with my own money," she cried. "It was the only new car I ever owned."

"Oh, Violet," my dad said from the backseat, "we'll get it fixed."

"No, we won't," she said, pointing to the steam that was bubbling up under the crumpled hood and rising in a thin wisp from the radiator. "It'll never be the same." Her hand shook as she undid her seat belt and grabbed her purse off the floor. Outside, cars were whizzing by without even slowing down or changing lanes.

"How are we going to get home?" Her voice sounded lost and childlike. She pulled on the door handle, and the passenger door cracked open letting in a rush of wind as cars roared past.

"We'll figure it out," I said. I had no doubt we would. For seven years I had been a road musician, touring in old buses, trucks, and vans on a less-than-zero budget. I'd found my way through more rollovers, accidents, and roadside breakdowns by the age of twenty-five than most people experienced in a lifetime. And that was before car insurance, roadway coverage, credit cards, and savings accounts.

"We'll have to get it fixed," I said in a disgusted voice. "We might have to rent a car and tow it."

"Tow it," she screamed. "We're over five hundred miles away from home." She pulled out her wallet and began digging through it. She pulled out a driver's license, an insurance certificate, and a roadway assistance card from the neat slots of her billfold. "You know what that would cost?" she said.

"Could I see those?" I asked, taking the cards from her hands and scanning them for information. For accident coverage, they had State Farm with a five-hundred-dollar deductible and no emergency tow services.

Rather than a AAA membership, like everyone else in the country has, they had Oldsmobile Roadway Assistance. I checked the paperwork, scanning through the list of twenty-five provisos, exclusions, and caveats, the most significant of which was the requirement that the car could only be towed by an authorized Oldsmobile dealership to the nearest Olds dealer. Otherwise, claims would not be honored. In this way, it seems, we belonged to General Motors forever.

My mother began to pull all the plastic cards in her wallet out one by one, as if an answer lay there. Her hands were shaking. From the driver's side, I noticed the contents of her wallet—a Social Security card, a lifetime membership in Sam's Club, an Amoco gas card, and a garden-variety MasterCard.

My mind began to reel. In my wallet, stashed on the floor of the backseat, I held my own secret lineup—a Gold-Plus AAA Card, a Preferred Gold MasterCard, and a Platinum Visa. Forget, *Don't leave home without it.* Hello, *Anywhere you want to be.* I knew I could get us home. The only challenge was how quickly and efficiently.

By now the contents of my mother's purse were spilling over her lap as she kicked open the passenger door with her foot, her hankies, lipsticks, and compact rolling onto the pavement.

"We need to get some help," she said, jumping out of the car with her wallet tucked under her arm.

"Oh, Violet." My father reached for his windbreaker. "Just wait a second." He slipped his arms into the sleeves. I reached into the backseat and grabbed my coat. The breeze that had seemed so cool and refreshing from the inside of the car was now blowing hard and cold on the outside.

By now, my mother was standing on the edge of the highway without a coat, waving her Oldsmobile Roadway Assistance card at passing motorists as if the sheer sight of it would cause automobiles to go from ninety to zero in five seconds flat. It wasn't working. Cars were switching to the left lane and zooming by to avoid this wild-haired madwoman hanging on the side of the road.

"Why won't they help us?" my mother screamed back at us in the wind. From the car, we watched her step into the driving lane and raise her arm again. All the cards from her wallet floated to the pavement.

"Violet," my father said with alarm. He jumped out of the car and rushed up the road to where she stood. I followed behind, collecting the glass, chrome, and fiberglass pieces of our car as I went along.

"Get out of the lane," my father screamed, waving his hands at my mother. He followed behind her, bending to pick up the cards as they blew down the highway. "You're going to get us all killed."

I finally caught up with them. In my arms I held a good selection of fragments from the Oldsmobile's front end. "Why don't you guys get in the car?" I said, dumping the pieces in a pile near the ditch. "I'll stay out here and try to get help."

"No!" my mother screamed, a cry raging in her voice. "Why won't they stop and help us?" I could almost hear her thinking, *People back home would never act this way.*

I circled around to the back of the car, picking up more debris, the bent rims and bits of glass from our headlights. I returned and added the pieces to the pile.

"They won't stop for all three of us," my father screamed over the wind. He pulled my mother toward the car. She finally yielded, but not before coming back to hand me the Oldsmobile Roadside Assistance card.

As soon as they were inside the car, a beat-up Chevy pickup slowed down, pulled to the side of the road, then snaked its way toward me in reverse with its backup lights shining. Inside it were the two guys with baseball caps, who quickly agreed that they would drive to the next town and call the highway patrol. I talked to them for a few minutes, telling them what had happened. I pointed down the road to where I thought the deer had landed.

"If you bag it," the one guy asked, "do they let you keep the meat?" He eyed the median where I had pointed, as if he were considering coming back and loading up the carcass himself.

"I don't know what they'll do with her," I said, looking down the road.

"Maybe they'll feed it to the wolves," the other guy in the baseball cap said.

Then I saw my mother open the car door and step out of the passenger side, her white shoe setting down on the pavement. "Don't forget," she leaned on the frame of the open car door and screamed in the wind. "Tell them that it has to be a tow truck from an *Oldsmobile* dealership."

After the two guys in baseball caps drove off, on their way to make the phone call for us, I knew that we'd have a long wait. I spent the time cleaning up the rest of the debris, running back down the highway about one hundred feet where a few large pieces of fiberglass lay in the middle of the road. Cars hurtled by, sending them flying in smaller pieces. After I gathered them all, I waited for the lanes to clear, then I charged across the road, and scanned the median for the deer.

I found her lying flat and completely still on her right side, her left eye blankly staring into the sky. I thought about how, for a moment before she disappeared from my view, just as the car had lifted her off the ground, I caught a glimpse of recognition in her eyes, as if she'd always suspected that we were out there, somewhere, speeding madly by on the edge of her world.

I climbed down into the grassy median and bent closer to her. She looked as if she had not moved or struggled in that spot, as if she had been dead when she landed. I hoped that was so.

I thought about something a friend told me about the writer Barry Lopez—how he stops when he sees road kill on the side of the highway, and he kneels beside it to bless the animal and ask for forgiveness. I considered doing it for this creature that I had killed but found I could not. Something inside me would not say I was sorry.

One thing you discover after you hit a deer is that nearly everyone else in the world has, or has almost, hit a deer. And when you try to tell your story to people, they will interrupt you with their own I-hit-a-deer stories.

Their stories may be more or less dramatic than yours, but they've had more time to formulate the plot, so they will rush ahead in the telling and leave you behind, holding that jumbled collection of details that you have not yet neatened into a story. In this way for a time, you will go away frustrated from the experience of hitting a deer.

That day after I cleared the debris from the road, I returned to the car and told my parents that I'd found the deer. I assured them that she was dead and that she appeared not to have struggled.

"I don't care about the damn deer," my mother said. "All I care about is my car."

I turned to look at this woman in the passenger seat. She had smoothed her hair down with a comb and applied a fresh coat of lipstick; it ringed her lips in a bright O. Her purse was reinstalled at her feet, packed up and all in order. For a second I had the urge to push my fist hard into her mouth, but I did not.

We spent forty-five minutes sitting in the car, waiting for the highway patrol, repeating the four or five things we knew for sure—how no one saw her coming, and that we'd been very lucky, how it could have turned out much worse, and how it was no one's fault. I found myself wishing that Nick were there; it wouldn't have happened to him. But both my parents made a point of saying they were glad I was the one who had been driving and that neither of them could have done a better job.

Then the highway patrolman arrived. He asked to speak to me alone in the patrol cruiser, since I was the driver. I gave him my parents' insurance certificate, and my driver's license. After he called the tow truck and filled out the accident re-port, he offered to give me a ride to town because the tow truck would only accommodate two passengers. My mom and dad agreed to stay with the car.

When I got to the Oldsmobile dealership, I knew I had about thirty minutes to devise a plan. I asked Jeff, the shop manager, if I could use a phone. He put me behind a desk, and I got to work, dialing numbers, calling insurance companies, inquiring about rental trucks. My idea was that we would strap the car into a tow dolly behind a rental van or truck and get on the road. We would be home a few hours later than planned, but still we would get there by evening.

I made careful notes, and I calculated costs. All told, it came to about two hundred dollars, a pittance, which I had decided I was going to pay if the trip-interruption insurance would not cover it. I did all this in twenty minutes and was beginning to feel quite proud of myself.

I was sitting with my feet up on the desk, thinking about a scene in an old movie called *The Hawaiians*. The film is an adaptation of a James Michener novel starring Charlton Heston as an imperialist settler of Hawaii, famous for having introduced the pineapple to the island.

In the movie, Heston's character becomes hugely wealthy and lives alone with his son in a large, plantation-style home. The mother of the boy has been dead for years, her portrait occupying a place of honor above the formal dining table.

For the most part, I've forgotten the movie, but there's one scene that's always stayed with me. Near the end of the story, when the son reaches his late teens, he grows restless with being the heir-apparent to the pineapple fortune and yearns for true adventure. There are a couple of heated scenes between the boy and the father, until Heston, an old sea man himself, realizes the boy needs to test his mettle in the larger world and arranges for his son to set sail as a ship's mate.

The next day seeing the boy off at the pier, the father knocks the kid on the side of the head and says in that Heston voice, "Son, take care of yourself." He grabs the boy's shoulders and stares at him face-to-face, as if he can't believe the boy will soon be a man.

"I will, Pa," the boy says obligingly and kicks the dirt.

"And if you get into trouble," Heston begins, but then he stops himself. He has all the power and wealth of the world at his disposal.

"If you get yourself in trouble," the father begins again, turning away from the boy and starting the long walk down the pier. The camera lingers on the back of his short-cropped riding jacket, as he yells, "Well, just get yourself out of it, that's all."

The day we hit a deer, I remember looking out the window of the body shop and waiting for my parents to appear in the tow truck. I was anxious to show them all my worldly gifts, the survival skills I had developed since they last knew me as a child.

Soon the tow truck pulled into the lot with the Oldsmobile trailing behind. It seemed strange to see the wreck so far from the freeway, trussed up in tow straps and traveling through the city as if on display.

"Oooh." Jeff, the body shop manager, winced and stepped away from the plate glass window when he saw the car. "That's bad."

My parents climbed down from the tow truck and walked across the parking lot. They looked small to me then, like children getting off a school bus at the end of a day full of pop quizzes and word problems.

They came through the door with that beaten look on their faces. I jumped to my feet and introduced them to Jeff. The body shop manager scratched his head and talked to my parents for a while, agreeing that, no, the car sure didn't look like it could be driven home, and adding, "Gee, it sure was strange that a deer was out there on the road at this time of the day."

My parents nodded. My father looked at Jeff with glazed eyes. "We didn't even see it coming," he said for the fortieth time.

"Well, here's the idea I have," I said, sensing the chitchat was winding down. I stepped out from behind the desk and began to spell out the plan, giving them details and dollar amounts. I could finalize the arrangements within twenty minutes, I told them, then Jeff would mount the car on the tow dolly, and we'd be down the road.

I stopped breathlessly and looked around.

"Did I mention," I said, "that I'm willing to pay for all this?"

It's not as if I expected them to jump up, clap their hands, and scream, "Oh, goody, goody, goody," like a couple of five year olds. What I wanted to see was a sigh of relief, the recognition that the crisis was over. Jeff stood off toward the corner watching the scene.

Then I noticed that my mother was shaking her head and, in fact, had been shaking her head all along. My father was silent, staring out the window, perhaps not hearing anything I had said.

"Oh, mercy, no," my mother said in a wary voice as if I'd told her some very bad news. "Oh, no," she repeated, her voice soft and wobbly.

I then realized that the plan had too many moving parts for her, too many components all strung together. For the plan to be a success every part had to function properly, and my mother never believed anything complicated would function properly, except sometimes maybe when it did so by accident.

Right there in the body shop, she was considering all the worst possible scenarios: What if the car came loose floating backward on the freeway, causing a twelve-car pile-up, which would be followed by just as many lawsuits? What if the rental broke down and then we'd be stuck in some strange town with a broken-down truck and a wrecked car?

"Oh, no," my mother repeated. Then she turned and walked toward the telephone.

"Let's call Nick," she said to my father. Right now Nick would be in the fields feverishly working late into each night, trying to get his crops planted in time to beat the coming rains.

"Nick could come and get us," my mother said, her voice lifting. She liked the sound of it already.

I looked at Jeff, the body shop manager. Maybe my eyes were saying, "Help me out here." But Jeff didn't answer. He drew a deep breath, raised his finger in the air and began to move toward the door.

"Tell you what," he said, "I'll give you folks a chance to talk in private."

I couldn't blame him. Who wouldn't like to be rid of a family and all the hurts and history they carried with them with one simple turn of a doorknob?

"Call Nick?" I said in disbelief as soon as we were alone. I couldn't believe what I was hearing. Every day my father drove out to the farm to hound my brother, quizzing him and cautioning him: Are you keeping up? How much did that cost? Don't buy that tractor. Stay ahead of the weather. Don't let the bank get a hold of you.

And now they were proposing that we pull him out of the field for two days during spring planting to come and save us.

"We're over five hundred miles from home," I said to my mother. It felt good to be the one reminding her of this. "It would take him ten hours just to get here."

"We don't have any choice," my mother said. She walked over to the desk, picked up the phone, and dialed my brother's number.

"Nick," she said, when she got him on the line. "We had a little accident." She paused while Nick said something on the other end. "We're all okay," she said, "but the car is wrecked." And now her voice got high and watery. "And we were wondering," she said, "if you could come and get us."

And so it was decided. My brother would arrive late that night with his Suburban and tow dolly. We would all stay in a motel, and in the morning he would take us home, driving a confident ninety miles per hour with the wrecked Oldsmobile in tow.

That afternoon, after everything was settled, we got a ride to a Comfort Inn on the south side of town. Once in the lobby, I stepped up to the front desk. As a former road musician, I had spent half my life checking in and out of motels. This was something I could do.

"Two rooms," I said and opened my wallet. "Nonsmoking." I pulled out the Platinum Visa. It felt good in my hands as I snapped it onto the counter.

"Oh, no." My mother stepped up behind me and looked for a moment at the silver Visa tucked under my fingers as if it were contraband. She smiled at the girl behind the counter. "We're all family," she said. "One room will do just fine."

"I'm happy to pay for this," I said. All I wanted was a bath, a bed, forty-five channels of mindless distraction, and a few hours of quiet.

"You can't afford this, honey," my mother said. She slid my Visa toward me on the counter. "You know you're not working right now." She opened her billfold to reveal a crisp row of twenties.

"Let her spend her money if she wants," my father said, fatigue in his voice.

He was near the front door, looking out the lobby window. He was scanning the cars in the parking lot, as if already expecting my brother to be there.

"We should be way past Miles City by now," my mother said in a confidential tone to the girl behind the counter, as if motel policy required that we must explain why we needed a room. "But our daughter hit a deer with our car." She gestured toward me, the culprit.

"A deer?" the girl behind the counter said, giving me a shocked look.

By this time, I'd moved over by the continental breakfast nook, but still my mother's voice followed me. "Our son is coming to get us," I heard her say, as I rounded the corner to the vending machines.

"We didn't even see it coming," I heard the echo of my father's voice say. And I was almost to the stairwell when the girl behind the counter began to tell my parents about the time that she almost hit a deer.

10

FAILURES OF THE HEART

The last thing I said to my father was "I'll be back," not in black leather with an Uzi slung over my shoulder like The Terminator, but like the daughter I was—the one who left home and didn't come back for years, the one who rarely called or wrote.

Although he was on the upswing and the charge nurse at the hospital in Bismarck had joked with him that he was the healthiest guy in the ICU, the place where he had landed when he flatlined three days earlier in another ward, he still had serious problems, three large blockages that would require surgery. I came to appreciate the impossible gauntlet he faced that last morning when the doctors arrived. "I want to go home" was his most repeated sentence, but without surgery, we all knew he would never see home again.

For days I'd been sitting in the hard-back chairs, staring through the long glare of fluorescence, thinking that before I left, somewhere in the middle of the hospital workers' coming and going, there might be a moment, some kind of exchange just between the two of us.

The talk would not be about dying. It would be about an old Packard he'd owned or a hard winter he'd endured. He'd raise his hand in the air and point in that abstract way up and to the right, to the place where all his stories came from, describing the slope and pack of the drifts that year, and then everything would be understood between us. And I would hold those words under my tongue like a gold coin, smuggle them out of the hospital, and put them on my dashboard like a St. Christopher medal for the long drive home, where I was certain upon my arrival to receive a phone call informing me of his death.

This was nothing that any of us talked about in the hospital, for we were best at talking around the edges of things. Mostly we spoke of our neighbors in the ICU—a young girl down the hall who had crashed her car into a bridge and was in an irreversible coma, and an old Greek man next door who was unconscious after a leveling stroke that had left him with a single, involuntary spasm—a loud and irregular hiccough that sounded like a dog barking. All day and night we listened to his yelps, and we talked with his wife, who was also old and Greek, and was incessantly using the ICU phone to make calls to places like Athens, Paris, and New York.

"Mr. Thompson died last night," we'd say in a whisper about a patient three doors down. He was an old farmer whose family I'd met in the waiting room the day before, just after he'd gone into heart surgery—the same surgery that our father was eventually going to need.

That night in the waiting room, the oldest son had told me his father had said to him before going into surgery, "I'll try like hell to make it through, but if I don't, I've had a good life." Maybe it was just the kind of thing you say at a time like that, mostly to comfort those around you, but I thought they were pretty good last words for an old man who had most likely spent much of his life outside of language, negotiating in grunts and curses with livestock and tractors.

You hear about eloquent last words—Goethe sitting up in bed, for example, saying, "More light," then falling back and expiring—and you hope that when your time comes you can enter the zone of death with some grace, if not physically then perhaps linguistically.

But our family said and did nothing profound or poetic in the face of death. As the news of Mr. Thompson's failed surgery hit us, it circled the room like a telegraph, lighting up with surprise on my father's face and resting there for one big who-me moment, until my mother picked out the coupon circular from inside the newspaper and commented on something she needed that was on sale at K-Mart.

At one point, my sister bravely stood by my father's bed and asked him if he was able to take any comfort in his faith. The answer, which I strained to overhear, was either "Not really," or "A little." Neither answer sounded encouraging to me. Could this be my father, who attended church every holy day and Sunday, who had carted me off to confession every

Saturday? Was I such a lavish sinner that I needed confession that often? I remember sitting in the passenger seat of the pickup as we bumped toward town, feverishly concocting sins to tell the priest: "I have lied seven times" (and in this number I would include the lie I had just made up about lying seven times); "I have disobeyed my parents" (I liked the rhythm of this); and "I am sorry for these and all my sins."

These days in the hospital room, a whole lifetime of churchgoing didn't seem to offer any of us answers. Where had all that catechism training gone? Instead I thought about Elisabeth Kübler-Ross's five stages of dying (we were vacillating between denial and bargaining, I suspected), and my mother vaguely recalled seeing a TV show about people who'd had near-death experiences—how they'd had this overwhelming impulse to go into the light. "They say you sometimes see relatives," my mother offered.

"Well, I haven't seen any," my father mumbled.

Most often those last days my father sat up in bed, looking perky even with his oxygen tube, his fluid drip, and his asymmetrically beating heart monitor. Even though the IVs in his veins were spreading purple bruises up his forearms, he still managed to joke about this, calling himself the human pin cushion and flirting with the nurse when she removed him from his bed for his daily bowel movement, saying, "Ah, she just wants to be alone with me."

But for all his bravado, it was impossible to ignore that he had begun to collect specialists—first, a cardiologist, then a kidney man, who guarded his fragile organs like a jealous lover—each doctor advocating the rights of his respective body part, the cardiologist arguing finally and importantly that improving the blood flow would benefit the whole system. Also on the crew was the internist who had reacquired my father's heartbeat three days earlier during the meltdown. This young doctor, having saved my father's life, now felt compelled to check on him, and we felt compelled to wave at him every time he passed by the door.

Most recently joining the team was a handsome intensivist, which I later learned was the title for someone who specializes in intensive-care medicine, and whom I later recognized as someone I had gone to college with. How strange to think of him, that big-haired sonorous tenor in choir in the seventies, now saving lives in a hospital smock and Dockers, in the nineties.

And how strange, at the foot of my father's hospital bed, for small talk about college days to ensue. And what was I up to, the intensivist asked out of politeness.

"Guarding punctuation standards," I replied.

In the bright hospital room, with machines humming and wheezing, with telephones ringing and crash carts beeping—someone in the background yelling, "Clear"—and the muffled names of doctors being paged in unknown codes, my job of scrutinizing the inscrutable semicolon didn't sound important, and certainly not significant enough to take me away from my father's hospital bed.

But I had work to do—my parents had raised me that way—and now I needed to leave. This had been my second eight-hundred-mile trip from Iowa to Bismarck in the ten days since the initial heart attack, and it was no longer possible to delay the progress of my students' lives. Each day that ticked off, my classes were producing papers I had not read. Finals, grading, and graduation were upon us. And no one in my family would have insisted that I stay.

At the very least, my father seemed pleased that I knew the intensivist personally, as if the family now had a medical insider and all the specialists would be newly invested in his care, maybe even breaking out the top-drawer, velvet-covered, under-lock-and-key treatment.

I once wrote a story called "Smokes" about a young woman (me, way back then) who was a road musician (which I was in my twenties) who comes home to visit her parents (mine) after a year-long road trip and little communication. The parents, surprised by her sudden appearance, greet her on the front stoop with their hands awkwardly at their sides, as if afraid she will try to sell them a Kirby vacuum cleaner. All of this really happened, but I realized after writing the story that they were mostly worried about the oil from their daughter's old car, which was likely to drip (and did) onto their newly poured concrete driveway.

In the story, "Smokes," you immediately know that the parents don't approve of the young woman's activities—the father watches TV with the remote in his hand while the daughter tries to tell them about all the tourist sites she's visited, thinking that if they are not interested in her touring, perhaps they will be interested in her tourism. But they are interested in neither. It is clear all this has been argued about and left unresolved between them years before.

So, what to do with a recalcitrant daughter—the father scans the channels, and the mother chats self-consciously about her part-time job. Eventually the young woman retires to her bedroom, which has been converted to a guest room in her absence. She spends the weekend with the crisp doilies and the ever-staring eyes of her mother's new porcelain doll collection.

Eventually the young woman repacks her failing car and the parents gather on the berm of the front lawn to wave good-bye. The father steps forward and leans into the front window, to kiss her good-bye, she thinks. But instead he slips a meticulously folded fifty-dollar bill into her palm and says, "Don't tell your mother."

The daughter wants to tell him everything then—about the married guitar player, about how the band cheated her out of her money and equipment, and about how she has nowhere else to go—but the father backs up and slaps the fender of the rusting car "like a palomino he's releasing into the wild," the story says.

Mostly the story is about the ends of ropes—the one the girl has reached, and the other she will reach for by the end of the story. It begins with the lines:

> Here at last is the short end of the long rope her father
> warned her she would eventually come to. "Long enough
> to hang yourself with," he had said, when he finally did
> say something to her that last time she went home.

It's a figurative statement I heard often growing up—giving someone a rope long enough to hang themselves with—

meaning, I've always thought, that it doesn't pay to rein some-one in, trying to make them do what you want them to do. They'll just chomp harder at the bit and hate you for pulling it tight. Better to give them some rope, let them have their own lead and a little head room. Eventually they'll do some-thing stupid with all that freedom and come back hang-doggy, newly penitent, and beautifully self-trained.

Writing about it now, I realize that the metaphor must originate in animal husbandry, perhaps horse training, and I imagine the technique works for the mildly stubborn horse. But what about the big, bad, wild one that I was as a young woman—headstrong, beautiful in my youth, wanting to blow off the doors and burn down the world, my neck stretched out to the absolute farthest reaches, my tongue out, my hair crazy in the wind, always breaking the rope's hold as it broke me.

These days I am haunted by the image of those sad dogs on long ropes you sometimes see in the yards of well-meaning owners, who perhaps want to give their pets roaming room during a long day away. But the long rope, whether given in love or discipline, is still a rope, and by the end of the long day, the poor animals are always hopelessly bound up, their feet and legs and neck all twisted and confused in the un-bearable length of it.

But what strikes me most, thinking about the long rope now, is the image it presents of the unbreakable connection we have with those we are born to—how those we are bound to can use it to hold, break, and ensnare us.

And how sometimes, too, it can be the only thing that saves us, our last and final safety net.

I once had a friend whose mother died the evening we were in night class together. When her roommates came to the classroom to get her, just to say something had happened, because nothing was known for sure, I still remember her sharp cry in the hallway and the way her legs buckled under her— that kind of pure cellular response. She didn't even come back to the classroom to gather her books. She ran out of the building, straight to her mother's bedside, which, I see now, is the absolutely right thing to do.

Not the way we were doing it—with me, standing by his bedside leaning in to say good-bye; and him, sitting up in his bed reading the morning paper, reminding me to check the fluid levels in my van—as if we were all back home in the kitchen and I was on my way to an out-of-town basketball game. I was almost out of the hospital room when I saw the team of doctors assembling outside the door, talking quietly and snapping charts open and closed.

I sat back down in the wooden chair. For days, we'd been waiting to hear what the doctors could do for our father, and getting on the road one hour later was not going to make any difference.

Seeing the white coats gathering in the hallway caused my father to raise the *Bismarck Tribune* higher, chunk out the creases with one swift motion, and bury his face in it, as if the story on which his life depended lay in its crinkly sheets.

It's a funny thing about the ICU. Each morning the new shift nurse pulls wide the swinging curtain, greets you, and puts the new date on the message board, like a blue star you've earned for being good. And each morning my father insisted on reading the newspaper front to back while we all sat vigil in a circle around him. Maybe it was the sheer assertion of regularity, for certainly he kept himself alive ten extra years simply by insisting on routine. Or maybe it was the comfort of looking in on the tragedy of others—that oh-no-not-me feeling. Pick your baddest bad day, and you're sure to find someone in the newspaper who's having an even worse one. So as my father's team of specialists filed in with the verdict on his tests and their strategies in hand, there he was, nose in the paper, impassively scanning the thin columns for someone else's disaster.

The cardiologist took the center position at the foot of his bed. With all the blood tests and EKGs and X-rays administered to it, a body is always trying to tell a story, and this doctor had read more chapters of my father's narrative than anyone else in the room. He'd maneuvered my father through the failings of his heart, and through the massive stroke eight years before that had left him paralyzed on one side and in rehabilitation for six months. He'd conferred on my father's prostate surgery, as well as the removal of a malignant growth and the recurring gout.

All his life, it seemed to me, my father had been this odd combination of fierceness and fragility—his body, small and failing; his mind, iron-willed and full of the angry teeth of survival. As an infant, he told me, he was once baptized in beer by a bunch of drunken uncles who christened him John. Perhaps it was fortunate that his mother stood firm and named him Felix, a name that means "fruitful" and "fortunate," for my mother insisted that, like the famous cat, he had spent at least all of his nine lives on his various health problems. There was the near brush with death at three when he contracted pneumonia, and the operation in his twenties when he'd had a tumorous lung removed at the Mayo Clinic, the place where all the famous sick people went. We were proud to have a dad who'd been sick enough to go to the Mayo.

When we were kids, we liked to sit behind him when he had his shirt off and trace the long pink scar that ran down his spine from the base of his neck then veered off to the left and under his shoulder blade like a twenty-four inch zipper. "Oh, that bugger itches," he'd say when a rainstorm was approaching. We were impressed—our father, the weatherman.

These illnesses created a pattern in my parents' relationship—our strong mother with her near-perfect health acted as the consummate doctoring partner for our stubborn father's failing health—just as she was now, standing beside his bed, to the left of the cardiologist, waiting to receive the latest news.

Flanking the heart man on either side were the kidney man and the intensivist. They weaved in their Italian shoes talking about dye tests, blocked arteries, triple bypasses, and stents, as my father listened coolly from behind his newspaper. He looked like a tiny, spoiled despot whose reluctant generals, fearful for their heads, were making report on the bad turns at the Peloponnesian Wars.

"I want to go home." My father sniffed apathetically and snapped the sports section.

"Well, we'd all like that for you." The cardiologist shuffled his shoes. This was a dance they had done before, I could see, and although the doctor was younger and had more training, my father was dancing for his life. He was cagey and punch-drunk like those people you see at the end of dance-a-thons, bug-eyed from being dragged around the floor for too many hours.

He'd had his first, very slight heart attack almost twenty years earlier. I remembered it vividly because for years I believed, and perhaps even now believe, I was the cause of it.

I recall I had just returned to the Midwest from a long road tour with my band during which I hadn't phoned them. Our conversations back then only escalated into arguments about how I was wasting my life. But one day, back in the region, I saw that we had a gig not far from my hometown, and with a little arranging I would be able to visit them for a few hours before going on to the performance.

I steeled myself and made the phone call. They were surprised but seemed happy to hear from me. We agreed that I would be there by dinner, and I set off on the road for the three-hour drive to their house. But when I arrived, my father was not home. He was in the Wishek Hospital, thirty miles south of my hometown.

In the three hours since I'd spoken to him, he'd had his first mild heart attack. It had begun with a tightness in his chest and a shortness of breath, my mother said, shortly after

I'd called. It was lucky he'd gone straight to the clinic in town, she said, because they'd been able to minimize the damage when the attack came.

Perhaps it was the narcissism of youth, but I'd never experienced that kind of direct cause-and-effect catastrophe before. I had experienced some weird coincidences—I might be thinking of someone, and the phone would ring and that person would be on the other end of the line. I often had problems with electromagnetic activity. Watches stopped on my wrist. Sometimes whole rows of streetlights blacked out as I walked or drove by them. I seemed to blow out light bulbs at a phenomenal rate, and often small electrical appliances smoked and died in my hands. But causing my own father's heart attack? This was getting scary.

And the situation got even more serious when I arrived at the hospital. I found him lying on his back on the hospital bed. He was prone and swaddled in white, still as a mummy. I'd only been there a few minutes, sitting quietly by his bed—I hadn't spoken a word—when the nurses came to remove me. My presence had made his heart monitors bing and bong with fibrillation. So much for the comfort of a loving daughter.

But all these years later, it was different. There was still a current that ran like a wild shot of 220 between us, but maybe our polarities had shifted. This time I felt my presence calmed him. Whenever possible, I tried to lean through the wall of machinery and touch him, to break down the barrier, and I noticed that no matter how bad he was feeling he lifted his head or pulled his body up to receive my kisses.

This was hard to believe from our brusque father, who would interrupt our stories when we were young with "Ah, you're just a dumb kid." It took me thirty years to figure out that this was his backhanded expression of love, the best he could manage without feeling foolish. Now here was our gruff father, reduced to a hospital bed and suddenly the willing recipient of our love.

That morning before the doctors arrived I had given him a foot massage. How strange to hold my father's small feet in my hands, and to feel how unmalleable they had become—his toes barely able to bend under my massaging fingers.

As soon as the team of doctors exited the room, off to other patients and other treatment plans, my father put down his newspaper and called for the nurses to bring him a dose of nitroglycerin. His throat was tightening, his head was getting light. The nurses put him in a reclining position and dimmed the lights. We all settled into chairs. I pulled up beside his bed and held his hand through the heart-racing moments, trying to visualize a calm feeling like waves of blue water spreading from my fingers through his body.

I contemplated calling my department chair and telling him to find a substitute to cover my classes through the end of the semester. Could I keep my father alive longer by staying, I wondered.

The poet Naomi Shihab Nye once spoke about asking her mother when she was young how you will know when you are about to die. "You are dying," her mother said, "when you are no longer able to make a fist." What surprised me about my father's hand that day was the power of his grip—how hard he was holding on. Was he holding on to me, or to life, I don't know. But I returned the grip, hard, like a mountain climber clasping a falling companion.

In "Smokes," my story about a road musician who goes home to visit her parents, after the father gives her the fifty-dollar bill and pats the rear of her car as it backs out the driveway—having nowhere else to go, the daughter leaves her small hometown and goes to the house of a friend in a nearby city. It's a big, communal, drop-in house, full of beaded curtains and partially furnished rooms with mattresses on the floors. She crashes there several weeks between bands, hanging out with the owner of the house, a leftover hippie named Freddie.

Very soon her money is depleted, and her car stops running. The action of the story turns on one afternoon when she and Freddie go through all their pockets, drawers, and glove compartments scavenging for a few coins to buy a pack of cigarettes.

The story is only partially true; I do remember lots of old hippie houses like Freddie's when I was young, and I did dig my fingers into the cracks of my old car seats once with my guitar player Greg. But I don't remember if we bought cigarettes with the money or a jug of Carlo Rossi wine or a Quarter Pounder. These were the only things, aside from guitar strings and pot, that we spent our money on in those days.

But the end of the story is all true—how the girl sits down and writes her parents a concession letter "in a weak and defeated hand," the story says. And that's exactly the way I remember it, written in pencil, barely audible, like a whisper dying on paper. The writer, who was me, weak with hunger and the sheer exhausting poverty of her life.

In the story, the girl sits back with the cigarette that she and Freddie have bummed from a neighbor, and she contemplates the ends of ropes—the figurative one she has reached and the literal one she will pick up later. With it, she thinks, "she will do something that will stun and amaze them all."

And that girl was me, who contemplated the rope and the razor blade, sitting in an efficiency apartment, out of work and out of money, three and a half months late on rent, and hiding, hunched over in the small closet when she heard the landlord's car pull up.

Her own car broken down. The phone disconnected. All the letters piling up in the mailbox, bills that she could not pay. And the knock that finally came, the one that knocked and knocked and would not go away, the voice that finally came around and called and called her name into the window, making it clear it was not her landlord—that was the voice of her father, come in person to answer her letter.

And he didn't say, "This is enough" or "Pack up, we're taking you home." He said, "Where's your landlord's house? Where's a good garage to fix your car? Where's the closest grocery store?" And he pulled out his wallet in a businesslike manner each time, towing my car to a garage, making arrangements with the mechanic to fix it.

And he walked down the grocery store aisles with me and stocked my freezer and refrigerator full, never once saying,

"Your life is a mistake" or "Get a job." Not that day, he didn't. And when he left me alone at the end of the day, he didn't say, "I love you." He simply handed me what I most needed—two hundred dollars in cash—and said, "Don't tell your mother," and it was never spoken of between us again.

A few years ago, on the way home from a New Year's Day party, I came upon a pickup in the ditch. It was late afternoon; there was just enough light to see that the tire tracks were fresh in the snow and we were the first people to pass by the scene. My friend who had gone to the party with me ran into the snowy ditch and looked in the cab. There she saw a man lying on his side on the seat.

Was he drunk, or dead, or dangerous? We were afraid to open the door, afraid of what we'd find, and afraid it might be some kind of trick. We were two women, out in the middle of a country road. But then we saw the lights of a house a few hundred yards up the road. So we got back in the car, raced to the house, and called 911.

Returning to the scene, we found someone else had stopped to help. The couple in the other car had already gone down into the ditch and pulled the man from the pickup. Now they shined a flashlight inside the cab, and you could see, in the better light, that the windshield had been smashed to cobwebs by the man's head. And as they brought him to his feet, I saw the fine lace of his cuts, such intricacy, with one long gash on his forehead, from which a heavy pulse of blood was spurting.

The scene was dizzying in many ways, but what stayed with me for hours was the blood that trickled down his nose and cheeks and pulsed from between his fingers as he covered his face in an attempt to stop the flow. Even in the half-light, as the blood fell in great long drips to the snow, it was a shade of red I had never seen before—not like the difference between orange red, or cinnamon red, or maroon red, but a red so vividly oxygenated and thrilled to be free of the artery that it literally cascaded down the man's face with each heartbeat.

Here was life expiring before us, we were certain of it. The couple that had pulled the man from the car set to work (amazingly, they had towels in their car) trying to staunch the flow. My friend and I stood around, wanting to help, but we were reluctant to put our hands in the man's blood.

"The ambulance will be here in minutes," we said to the couple. "We shouldn't move him."

But the couple had the man, who was tall and dazed, perhaps a bit drunk, up on his feet. "We need to get him to the hospital right away," they screamed.

"But the ambulance is on the way," I screamed back.

"But my car is right here," the driver said, and he folded the bleeding man into the backseat.

When we got back in our car and headed toward town, my friend and I talked on and on about our response to the accident, feeling ashamed that we wouldn't touch the blood for fear it was tainted. "If only I'd had a pair of rubber gloves," my friend said. She was studying to be a physician's assistant, and if something had really gone wrong, she might have been the only one to know what to do.

As we drove to town, a few miles down the road, we saw the ambulance we had called, all its lights flashing, screaming by us toward what had been the accident site. I realized then that all this had happened in less than ten minutes, and it struck me how quickly a life can change. One moment you're driving down the road, going home from a hot toddy party, and the next moment your life is spilled out on mile marker 27.

What mobilized us, I realized, what got us running for ambulances, and breaking down doors, and throwing half-unconscious drunks in our clean backseats, was that unearthly gush of red—how sure it made us that an emergency was at hand. But what about the rest of us bleeders, the ones whose lives are spilling out, so invisibly, each day?

I think about those weeping students I sometimes see on the concrete benches of the university where I teach, hunched over with their faces in their hands. Is it unpaid bills, or failed tests, or bad lovers that make them cry?

Passing one of them one day, my friend said to me, "You always hope you can make it home before losing it like that." And it is true. Now that I am one of those public bleeders, I see them everywhere—waiting in the bus shelter after a hard day with their lunch pails in their laps, or in their cars staring at a stop light with their hands resting on the steering wheel. And what is the appropriate response, I wonder? Sit down and ask what's the matter, offer a tissue, put your hand on the weeper's shoulder? Surely that would be presumptuous.

Yet I can't say how many times I have wished for some stranger to see that transparent pulsing-away in me, to correctly diagnose my advanced state of grief and put a hand on my hand, put an arm around my shoulders—to save my life some afternoon with a simple gesture—for grief happens in odd places, when one's friends are not around.

And even this is not fair to my friends, whose phone calls I stopped answering, whose invitations I declined. Since my father's death, I have grown selfish in my grief, not wanting to share it, only wanting to be alone in it. Wanting to be alone as I feel, and alone as I feel I deserve to be.

My father did not die the day I left him at the hospital, the day I leaned into his ear and whispered, "I'll be back." Although I never saw or spoke with him again. Two days later he underwent the least invasive form of surgery the doctors could offer. They installed a stent in his most severe blockage, and, afterward I'm told, he felt better than he had in years. He made it home, as he had always wished, but he was weak from the surgery. He lived for fifteen more days, steadily recovering until complications developed from the stent.

My mother recalls the best afternoon he had, when the weather turned sunny and warm, and he was able to sit on the front porch and talk with people as they came by. But mostly it was a cold and wet spring and he was forced to stay inside, probably watching TV, as he'd spent much of his time in those last years, and waiting for the nurse to come around for his daily checkup.

During those last two weeks of my father's life, I went back to work, finishing up the school year, and busying myself with the summer session, which began immediately after spring finals. I don't recall what else I did during those two weeks—slept and ate, watched the NBA playoffs, graded student papers, perhaps read a little.

I kept up with my father's progress through my sisters, who updated me periodically from the states where they lived. I do know that I never picked up the phone to call him, to ask him how he was doing. I never got in my car and drove the eight hundred miles or got on a plane and flew home to see him one last time—and for this I don't have an answer why.

What did he think about, alone in that big house those last two weeks? Did he wait for me to return, as I had promised, or at least to call? I doubt it—he'd understood long ago the kind of daughter I was.

But did he secretly wait for me to come to the door, to knock and knock and call his name, to pull tight between us, one last time, the slender unraveling threads that tied us to one another.

One day when my mother had to run errands, she left him alone for several hours, and when she returned he said in a small voice, "Boy, the days sure are long." I am haunted by these words. They are like a paring knife, twisting out the core of my heart.

How might I have eased and shortened the length of those last days, if only I had gone home to be with him? What other last words might have passed between us, I wonder, if only I had called. And what in all the world was so important that it kept me away? I cannot imagine now what it might have been.

11

SIGNS AND WONDERS

My sister Jane is now the mayor of my small hometown. She also manages The Korner, a long, narrow bar on the middle block of Main Street with a pool table, a row of high stools, and a large hall in the back where people hold wedding and anniversary receptions.

Jane's business card displays her full name along with her title, "Mayor," engraved in silver letters. In the lower left-hand corner of the card, she's listed the bar's number, along with the words "Call for Reservations" as if it's within her mayoral purview to make the entire town available for rent.

One summer a few years ago when I was home for a visit, I dropped by the The Korner to see her. She was busy in the back kitchen preparing a meal for what appeared to be thousands. She had boiling pots on the stove, ovens full of roasting chickens. She stood at the counter, churning a gigantic wooden spoon in a vat as she added hard-boiled eggs, mayonnaise, and salt to the potato salad.

"You'll never guess what I just found out," she said the moment I walked in the door. No "Hello." No "When did you get home?" Never long on preambles, Jane just picked up the conversation wherever we left off whether it had been months or years.

"Now what?" I asked, excited to have this inside information.

She stopped spooning potato salad and leaned back against the counter. She shook a Marlboro from its pack and put it to her lips. Her fingernails were long as scissor snips and polished a jet-engine red. I waited as she flared a lighter at the end of the cigarette then took a long, delicious drag.

"There's a river flowing under the whole goddamn town," she sputtered, her words coming out in one long plume of smoke.

That morning, she explained, a crew of state workers had been repairing a deep vertical crack in a storm drain on the south side of town. They'd closed off the street, broken through the pavement with jackhammers, and were opening a deep hole around the cracked drain with a hydraulic digger when they pierced the upper shell of what appeared to be an underground river.

The water had rushed into the excavated hole with such force that the digger's power shovel had been pushed away. Workers scrambled onto the street level as the hole filled. This is when my sister, the mayor, was summoned.

She described how she stood with the state workers around the new pond, which had capped off and was now overflowing into the street and the gutters. Everyone scratched their heads. Where was all this water coming from?

The foreman had retrieved a geological map of the state from his truck and unfolded it onto the hood of her car. My sister bent over the map with him and looked at the spot he pointed to—our town, tucked into the western edge of Logan County where the map indicated a large body of underground water.

"The water table is high this year," he said, pointing at the overflowing hole. "Otherwise, we'd never have tapped it."

"Do I need to build an ark?" Jane had asked. This was during her first term, when she was still feeling responsible for her citizenry.

"Not yet," the foreman said, folding up the map. "But you might want to think about buying the lumber."

"Who knew?" Jane said to me, crushing her cigarette in the ashtray and returning to her vat of potato salad. "There's water all around us."

We could laugh about this because the crisis was over. By noon, the crew had filled in the pierced upper shelf and forced the water back underground so that they could resume their repair work.

But for a long time after I learned this news, a strange feeling welled up in me, a kind of somber wonder. The sad part of me realized that this dust-filled place I had known as a child, the dry place of kicking rocks down gravel roads, would be hard to reconcile against this new image of a burgeoning green land teeming with underground rivers.

The other part of me, the wonder part, felt vindicated. Hadn't I always sensed some untamed thing rumbling beneath our feet?

Sometimes I feel like Hansel and Gretel, fumbling around in the dark for clues that will lead me home. In the quiet aisles of the university library where I teach, I search through *The Handbook of Functional Plant Ecology.*

I have followed this trail into one of the most remote and unpopulated tiers of the Parks Library, to find this botanical text. When I study the index, I find what I'm looking for— alfalfa, *Medicago sativa*—ranked as number seven on the list of the ten deepest root systems in the world. With roots that have been documented to plunge to depths of forty meters in search of water, alfalfa is the only plant on the top-ten list whose habitat is an agricultural field.

Of all the crops my father grew, only alfalfa sustained its deep green leaves, almost oily, almost succulent, through the hot, dry summer in central North Dakota. Technically a legume, alfalfa blooms yellow or fuchsia in some places, but it bloomed a soft blue-violet where I grew up and sprouted leaves that held a bitter olive color through the growing season.

The other plants included on the list of longest root systems are desert, forest, and woodland species, the hardiest in the world: the juniper (roots to sixty-one meters), which grows in the Colorado plateau; the eucalyptus (forty-five meters), which grows in places like Australia and the Jarrah forest; the acacia (sixty meters) and the shepherd's tree (sixty-eight meters) both of which grow in the Kalahari.

The body of a plant has two major parts: what we see above ground, the stalk, stems, leaves, blossoms; and what we do not see, the root system below ground level. Often in drier climates more biomass must be dedicated to the root system to go in search of water and nutrients.

Botanists have observed that plants evolve as they strategize their survival in different environments. They distribute their biomass accordingly. In an arid environment where ground resources are scarce, a plant will often scrimp on foliage, producing more modest displays of leaves and blossoms, balancing its need for photosynthesis and pollination against its need for ground resources.

If you want to survive in a dry place, if you want to go shamelessly green in the middle of nowhere, you must emulate alfalfa. If you want to bloom vividly, you must learn to put down a taproot that plunges to phenomenal depths in search of sustenance.

Alfalfa is self-reliant, a perennial whose leaves carry a nitrogen-fixing bacteria that enhances the plant's survivability in any soil type. And it is wily: The bud of alfalfa's flower trips its keel on the head of a foraging bee to maximize the spread of pollen.

Considered to originate in Iran, it spread to Greece in 490 BC with the Persian army who fed alfalfa to their horses, believing it made them swifter. Perhaps this is true—cows will never move so quickly as when they're headed for an alfalfa field. The normally placid bovine is known to go wild in its presence, eating and eating, tearing and chewing its leaves until the animal bloats. One grazing manual sternly cautions, "Do not turn hungry cows onto lush alfalfa pastures."

In a good year in North Dakota, this crop can be cut twice in one growing season, and up to three and four times in wetter regions with longer growing seasons. Sheared to within inches and harvested in midsummer, alfalfa will grow back to a full height to be harvested again. When farmers are swathing the fields, the acrid sweetness announces itself everywhere—in your clothes, your hair, your nostrils.

Once the field is cut, alfalfa's leafy stalks are bound up in bales. But it does not go easily. Alfalfa bales are the heaviest you will ever lift. You will sweat and swear. As you heave the bundles onto the flatbed, the twine binding will cut your hands. The weight will destroy your back. Once you have lifted it, your body will never forget alfalfa.

When the bales are stacked in the hayloft, the sweet smell fills the barn. The bales take months to dry, and even when you break one open in the middle of winter to feed the cattle, you will discover that inside, alfalfa never truly gives up its green.

The summer after my sister told me about the river flowing under my hometown, I visited the State Geological Survey office in Bismarck to consult an expert. With a state geologist, I studied the map of North Dakota. He pointed out the geological high points of my county—the rocky moraine left by the Wisconsinan glaciation, and the Missouri Coteau, a hummocky plain that overruns my county as it passes diagonally through the state.

He described to me the unique beauty of the place where I grew up. Although I imagined he saw all places as geologically interesting, I admired his gentle patience. I had barged into his workday without notice or appointment, and he had taken time to answer my simple questions.

Then he traced his fingertip around the circle of pink on the map that marked the caverns of water under my hometown. It was not a river at all, he explained. Instead, it was a glacial outwash, a system of springs and cisterns and finger streams—a permeable honeycomb of stratified sand and gravel through which water can filter.

"More like a sponge than a river," he said.

As indicated on the map, the underground glacial outwash spread miles around my hometown. But looking further, I was surprised to learn that the entire area that constitutes my family land is marked, not as farmable till, but as a hydrologic feature, a massive above-ground lake.

It's called Lake McKenna on the topographical maps, but we always called it West Lake. Only vestiges of it remain on the southern and western edges of town. North of town across Highway 34, bordering my brother's farm, is another isolated remnant of the big lake shown on the map. This pond is mostly shallow and reed-filled, too boggy for swimming, but Dad used to clear it of snow with the front loader in the winter when the water froze over, and it was excellent for ice skating.

At home, we just called it "the lake," probably because it was too close and familiar to warrant a proper name when we spoke of it between us, in much the same way as Midwesterners refer to Minneapolis–St. Paul as "the cities." Paris may be Paris, and Rome may be Rome, but Minneapolis–St. Paul will always be "the cities."

In addition to the small remnant of a lake on the edge of our farm, we had patches of open water moving along a direct northerly line on our property—a series of sloughs and springs that rose and fell depending on the season and weather. We always thought of them as independent anomalies, low pockets of standing water that refused to dry up in an otherwise productive wheat field.

My father saw them as pure nuisance, wasted acreage. But now on the geological map, I saw that they were all connected underground, and that our entire farm, above and below the ground, belonged truly to the world of water, and that it was just on loan to us.

Years ago, my brother took a photograph using a special mirror-filter on his new camera that created the illusion of the farmhouse surrounded by water. The house appears twice in the photo—first, high and dry, perched on the hill; and second, as a shimmering reflection in the glassy surface of the watery pasture below.

I always thought he'd created a trick lake because, landlocked as we were, he yearned for a real lake, but now I wondered if my brother had sensed all along the water coursing deep below our land, and if this photograph was a manifestation of his intuitions.

"Why didn't we learn these things in school?" I asked the state geologist. Maybe we had been taught them and the specifics hadn't pierced my distracted teenage consciousness. "If I had known that I was growing up in such an interesting place," I said, "I think I would have loved home a little more."

Did I mention that the geologist was a handsome man? Oh, he was handsome. He turned to look at me when I asked this question, and I think I saw his dark brown eyes mist over. I realized then that being a geologist must be lonely work— to fall in love with shale and sediment and topography, to spend your days unearthing the deepest layers of glacial history and hold it in trust for an oblivious and ungrateful society that lacks interest in anything below the slightest surface.

Signs and Wonders. People always remember Hansel and Gretel's lostness, how they dropped bread crumbs to leave a trail through the forest as they walked, and how the birds ate the crumbs. But few people remember the earlier part of the story—Hansel's cunning the first time their parents attempted to abandon them in the woods.

That first night, when Hansel and Gretel overheard their parents' anxious conversation about the lack of food in the house and their plans to lead the children deep into the forest at first light, Gretel despaired, but Hansel made a plan. He waited for the household to fall asleep then went outside and filled his pockets with white pebbles that glistened in the moonlight like silver coins.

The next morning when the children were led into the forest, Hansel dropped the shiny pebbles as he walked. As night fell in the middle of the forest, Hansel and Gretel waited for the moon to rise then followed the shiny path back to their home.

When the children surprised the parents the next morning by emerging from the woods unscathed, the father and stepmother acted relieved. But the second night, after the stepmother convinced the father to try it again—only this time taking the children deeper into the woods than they had ever been before—the stepmother proved her true wickedness by bolting the door before going to sleep. So Hansel was unable to go outside and refill his pockets with stones. The next morning he dropped bread crumbs, improvising with the only thing that was left to him.

It's easy to get lost in thought about the cruelty of Hansel and Gretel's parents, especially the spinelessness of the father who won't stand up to the stepmother and protect the children of his first wife. And one could wonder endlessly about why Hansel and Gretel would even want to return to this unfriendly home. But home is home, as the experts tell us, and no matter how bad it gets, we will yearn even for the rough familiar.

Besides, Hansel and Gretel know something we don't, something alluded to beyond the borders of the told story—how happy they were before their mother died, before the events that precipitated the stepmother's arrival in their lives. They remember that first father and they wait for his return.

So when we encounter Hansel and Gretel in the troubled middle of their tale, they're holding out hope, working backward, searching for an elusive trail of bread that will lead them back to some idea of home they vaguely recall.

Perhaps it's true that, as Thomas Wolfe wrote, "You can't go home again." Mostly because, as in Wolfe's case, after you write about the place you're from, people are waiting at the city gates with pitchforks and burning torches the next time you try to visit.

But another reason you can't go home again is that the shape you made upon leaving does not match your shape upon return. Not even for a weekend is it comfortable to step through the ill-fitting hole that your exit created and take up residence in your old life.

But return you must, if only in imagination. For if it's true that you can't go home again then it must be equally true that you can't *not* go home again. Your home ground has left an indelible imprint on you. "It is the landscape you learn before you retreat inside the illusion of your own skin," Scott Russell Sanders wrote. "You may love the place if you flourished there, or hate the place if you suffered there. But love it or hate it, you cannot shake free. Even if you move to the Antipodes, even if you become intimate with new landscapes, you still bear the impression of that first ground."

A few years ago, just as I was finishing graduate school, I attended a conference on Great Plains history and culture where I met Mary Defender-Wilson, a storyteller of Dakotah-Hidatsa heritage. In the hotel lobby waiting for a cab, we struck up a conversation about the places where we were from.

When I told her I was from a small North Dakota town east of the Missouri River, she quickly told me that this was also the place her ancestors had once called home. In fact, she said, some generations of her family were buried around there on a mound, near a creek. Our conversation became more engaged as we tried to identify her family's burial place, to match it against where my family's land was and where my own dead were buried.

She offered me descriptions—a series of hills, a rise in the path, a curving stream. I answered her with place names— Bryant Township, Logan County, Lake Isabel, Highway 3. We leaned in and laughed at our fumbling. Try though we might, we could not locate our common place, so effectively had my history overwritten the memory of her family's place on this land.

"We found the American West a curious place, alien and bare to our ears," Richard Manning wrote in *Grassland*. "Because of this, we failed to allow it to tell us its story, to give us its name."

Around the same time I finished graduate school, worrying about where I would go next, I had a dream in which I was driving across an unending countryside of unfenced grassy hills, en route to a large flint monolith I could see in the far distance.

As I was driving, a disembodied voice in the car commanded, "Turn around. You're on hallowed ground."

I responded to the voice, cranking the wheel so quickly that the car began to roll and I was thrown from the car. When I woke up in the dream, I was lying on the ground hugging the curve of one of the rolling tan hills. The grass was dry and prickly, the color of a bear cub's belly.

When I finally stood up, I could see that I was indeed on hallowed ground. A line of demarcation started directly at my feet. From that point forward for as far as it was possible to see the ground was encrusted with flat stones like jewels in the rolling surface of the hills.

I bent down to look at the rocks more closely, and I saw that they were about an inch thick—flat pieces of sandstone and marble and granite carved into the intricate shapes of letters. The entire landscape before me was strewn with them. I understood in one flash—in the way it's possible to do in dreams—that this was my oeuvre, my entire body of work revealing itself to me, observable for only this moment in one glance, and that I would spend the rest of my life working this field, arranging these letters into words, sentences, paragraphs.

I really began to cry then as I took in the enormity of the task, but what overwhelmed me even more was that many of the letters were carved into the shapes of alphabets I did not know. And some were carved into the shapes of alphabets not known to the modern world.

Fortunately, at this moment I woke up, just as you're often roused from a falling dream right before you hit the pavement. When I woke up, I found I was actually crying. I didn't stop for some time.

After that, I began to wonder if these hills actually existed in the physical world. If so, what was their geographic location? Every time I'd meet someone from a place I'd never seen—North Carolina, Nova Scotia, Israel—I would say, "Do you, by any chance, have rolling hills that are tan and round as a bear cub's belly?" It sounded ridiculous, but I wanted to know. I had an idea that this place was seeking me.

Then one time driving back to North Dakota on summer break, I decided to take the southern route home using the smaller highways rather than the interstate, cutting across the countryside. As I approached the moraine that runs by my hometown, I could see that all the rolling hillsides were encrusted with glacial debris. For miles and miles, they were embedded with flat stones that sparkled in the bright afternoon sun.

Meaningful work, my father once told me, is something I should never hope for. "There's work you'll do for free because you love it, and there's work you'll do to earn a living." Hard words for an eleven-year-old to hear, but I had asked the question: Did he enjoy being a farmer?

We had just spent a day picking rocks. All seven of us laboring under the hot sun, digging our fingers in the earth to pull free the small boulders that had surfaced in our plowed fields since last year. We would huff and complain under the weight of the rocks, then ride home on the stone boat at the end of the day, our clothes and faces dusty, our fingernails caked with dirt from the fields.

It was impossible work, but even I knew it was necessary. If we didn't clear the new rocks each year, they would break the plow disk during planting or the combine at the most inopportune moment during harvest. But I was curious about this constant movement of rocks. As we pried and shoveled and clawed, I continued to ask: Hadn't we cleared this field last year and the year before? Where was this endless supply of stones and boulders coming from?

These questions remained rhetorical because no one in my family cared to entertain them in the hot afternoon sun. We busied ourselves with hauling the rocks to the grassy corner of the north quarter, the spot chosen by my great-grandfather eighty years before. In this way, we followed patterns set in motion decades before we were born.

How strange it seems to me now, an adult woman so far from that life on the farm, that the struggle I face each day when I approach my writing desk—to bring to language the stories pushing up beneath my feet—feels so much like the hard labor of unearthing those half-exposed rocks in my father's fields.

And no matter how fiercely I struggled to evade my fate as a farmer's wife, becoming a writer instead, how strange it is to realize that writing, the act of arranging language in neat horizontal furrows, is a great deal like farming.

Still I am tempted to turn away from the work. I want to idle the tractor into the shed and turn off the engine; I want to drop a small boulder on my toe so that I can hobble home to bed and a good book, but curiosity keeps me at my desk. I slow down, turn to the larger questions: Where has this story been hiding? What forces drove it to the surface today?

The memoirist Patricia Hampl calls this *dwelling:* "I have come from people who have always been polite enough to feel that nothing has ever happened to them. They have worked, raised families, played cards, gone on fishing trips together, risen to grief and admirable bitterness and, then, taken patiently the early death that robbed them of a brother, a son. They have not dwelt on things."

"I have dwelt, though. To make a metaphor is to make a fuss," Hampl wrote. "I'm after junk. I want to make something out of what my family says is nothing."

My father never approved of my life on the road. He worried about my safety, my interrupted education, my financial solvency. I suppose he worried about my ruined reputation.

"No one will marry you," he'd say.

A few years after I graduated, one of my first rock bands was invited to play for my high school's prom. The night before, we were booked to play another prom in Rosebud, South Dakota, then we packed up our gear and drove though the night to get to Napoleon. We reached our farm just as my parents were getting up to milk the cows.

We parked the tour bus beside our farmhouse and slept away the day. My mother made us pancakes when she came in from chores. She made us spaghetti in the afternoon when we rose from sleep.

The prom turned out to be an extravaganza—mirror balls, fluorescent streamers stretching the length of the auditorium.

Strobe lights pulsed, cameras flashed, and balloons fell from the rafters as couples with big hair, tuxedos, and chiffon dresses walked down the aisle.

We performed from the stage in our usual manner: steeped to the teeth in leather; large stacks of amplifiers piled behind us; a fog machine blowing a crazy haze; flashpots popping off around us; 120 decibels of metal screaming at 120 rpms.

But what I remember most from that night is the face of my father, lost somewhere in the sea of faces, that anonymous crowd of parents with cameras relegated to watch from behind the wall of streamers—the outer edge around the circumference of the prom.

The view of my father's face that night remains clear to me, as if lit by a spotlight, and his expression was one of worry. Why did we have to play so loud? Was this really music? Did we ever comb our hair? And now it was certain, he was thinking, no one would ever marry me.

I was singing when my father died. A Saturday, nine years ago. I was in my living room with my guitar player rehearsing for a performance. "When will I see you again, a fire burns on your horizon," I was singing when I heard the phone ring.

I did not pick up the phone. We had a gig that night and our entire repertoire to review. "When will I see you again? Just tip your hat so I know that we were friends."

We finished practicing, and my second oldest sister called later, going down the list of people my mother hadn't yet reached to deliver the news—our father had died one hour before.

In all the confusion that followed, I forgot about my messages. When I checked the machine hours later, I heard five seconds of crackling silence, then the smallest whimper—my mother's voice, I've always assumed—followed by the receiver crashing into the cradle.

My father was a confident singer with a good sense of pitch. His timbre was light and reedy. It was easy to pick him out in church. He was the guy with the loud voice three pews back singing the crazy tenor parts. Even on the days when there were no altos or baritones in attendance at the early mass, he held to his tenor part, sounding even more wildly out of context. "Praise God from whom all blessings flow," he'd intone, a lone sheep crying in the wilderness. We would blush and hide our faces behind our chapel veils, but he would sing on. "We shall come rejoicing, bringing in the sheaves."

My father valued invention. The obvious bored him. A kiss on the cheek, any overt expression of love made him blanch with embarrassment. And he could be curt. When talking with him on the phone, you had to be careful to get the important news out quickly, because he would exit a phone conversation when he deemed it finished.

You might hear a small grunt, something like, "Yeah" or "Okay," then the line would click, and the hum of the dial tone would follow.

"Dad." You'd be left holding the dead receiver. "Dad, Dad?"

Right after my father's funeral, a family friend rushed up to me in the vestibule of the church. She was a pianist whose polka band had played wedding dances when I was growing up.

"Oh my," she said, when I turned to face her. "I never noticed before how much you look like your dad!"

Where does family resemblance begin, I wonder. In the shape of the eyes, a gesture, a tone of the voice? Is it in the turn of a phrase, the timing of a joke, a certain way of using the hands? I know from all these things that I am my father's daughter.

"I had to tell you," the woman said, "that your father was always so proud of you."

"Excuse me?"

"Your dad," she said, "he was always so proud that you stayed with your music."

"What?" I said, my eyes beginning to water. Could she possibly be speaking of my father, Felix, the one who would say, *Before you're old enough to draw social security, you should consider getting a real job.*

"Yes," she continued. "He talked about you and your music all the time."

Right there, in front of her, I started to cry then, not for me, but for my father. I saw he had been a Janus figure all his life, with two contradictory faces. The one side, the parental face, felt compelled to turn itself to me and say, "Settle down, stop all of this foolishness." The other face, the thwarted artist, hid itself from my view, but secretly rooted for me at every turn.

Since my father died, I've been finding dimes. On jogging trails, in corridors of hotels, several times at odd hours on the sidewalk leading to my office building at the university where I teach. I don't expect anyone to believe this.

At last count, I've picked up sixty-four in the nine years since my father's death. They collect on my writing table in two etched liqueur glasses. Eight more dimes ride on the dashboard of my car with my sunglasses, the lucky ones I found while traveling that never made it back to the liqueur glasses.

Twenty or so more dimes hide in my coats and suit jackets—I rediscover them when I reach into my pocket while teaching or singing. I've picked these up along the path and have neglected to deposit them in the glasses. About twelve dimes sit in a shot glass on the counter of my friend's apartment because after he met me a few years ago, he started finding dimes. And now my niece and my mother have begun to find them.

But how did it begin? Immediately after my father's funeral, the house was full of cousins, babies, old people, young people. I wondered who would dare to sit in his chair—a La-Z-Boy so thoroughly his that it retained a small oil spot on the upholstery where he rested his head in the end when he was too sick to go out.

No one sat in his chair that day. People milled around it, crowded together on the couch, creaked on the folding chairs. The La-Z-Boy remained unoccupied, except for a single, silver dime that rested in the center of the cushion all afternoon. I never picked it up, but the image of that thin flash of silver against the green upholstery stayed with me.

After that, the dimes began to appear. In my tally, I don't include the one I saw that first day, or the dozens I saw lying around in the months after my father's death, before I realized that I was finding dimes. At some point, I picked them up and began counting.

Sometimes they come in rushes or clusters—three, for example, in a neat pile under a table at the St. Louis airport one stormy morning after a turbulent early flight during which, flying through torrents of rain and great flashes of light, I felt compelled to ask several times, "Just exactly what happens when a plane gets struck by lightning?"

I never got the answer or my morning coffee because the pilot had instructed the nervous flight attendants to stay in their seats. I exited the plane, shaky-legged and determined never to fly TWA again, not even to board my connecting flight to Reno. The dimes were in a tiny pile on the newly mopped floor, directly beneath my table when I sat down to eat my breakfast.

To be fair, I never pick up the dimes I see around parking meters or in bars or other places where people might be distracted or inebriated or fumbling with their change. Sometimes I see a shiny thing on the ground, I also must confess, and when I reach to pick it up it's only a bottle cap or a gum wrapper. Sometimes, I can go for months without finding one.

Then one Christmas Eve day, I'll be feeling especially sad because of all the holiday music, and I'll lose one of my favorite earrings while shopping for last-minute presents. And when I backtrack to Pier One and rap on the darkened windows and question the custodial staff who've just swept the floor, and I am told, very patiently by these workers who just want to get home to their families, that they did not see a delicate silver earring shaped like a leaf with a small pearl, I will feel disheartened when I go back to my car, which in my haste I've left running in the middle of the parking lot with the headlights on.

The snow will be slashing at angles through the headlights as I'm sitting there feeling bad about Christmas, when I see something shiny flashing in the parking lot just ahead of me, in the very spot where I had parked hours earlier. And when I get closer, I'll be amazed to discover my lost earring, looking pristine and not stomped on or crushed by tires, and then when I bend down to pick it up, I'll see something else shiny below. And when I clear the snow with my gloves, I'll discover, suspended in a thin layer of ice directly below the spot where my earring had landed—one thin dime!

More signs and wonders. The Monday morning after my father died, I met with my summer class to tell them that I'd be leaving town for a few days for his funeral. My students were appalled that I had bothered to come to class. What is the appropriate thing to do when someone you love dies— tear your clothes, lie down and kick and scream, or quietly go on with assigned tasks? I still don't know. All I could think of was that my students had essays due that morning, and I didn't want to disappoint them by not showing up to collect them.

After I dismissed the class, one student came up to tell me how sorry he was about my loss. He was an older, long-haired student, one of my favorites because he had actual life experiences to write about.

Now he wanted to confess something. The essay he had written was about his father. He was proud that he had written about how much he loved and valued his father, but now he hesitated to turn in the essay. He worried that reading it might sadden me.

"No," I said, gathering my papers, "don't worry. I'll be happy to read it." Then I looked up at the student. He was wearing a baseball cap, and instead of the usual Nike logo, the hat read, "Felix" in bold letters, beside an illustration of Felix the Cat.

I stared at it in disbelief. "Where'd you get that hat?" I asked.

"Oh," my student said, tugging at the cap's bill. "I've had it for years. I never wear hats, but I just felt like putting it on this morning."

There was a pause between us. "Felix was my father's name," I said, and I saw my student's face go white. My father was always a trickster in life.

One dime found in a plate glass window, suspended behind a dusty cardboard poster in the front window of a store where I stopped to use the bathroom. Dimes on deserted walking trails through the woods. Dimes in bathroom hallways, in elevators, under theater chairs. A dime resting on top of my computer tower, where there was no dime ten minutes before. One dime on the silver tray of the checkout counter where I go to buy office supplies.

In another store, a woman fumbles with her money, and I wait behind her, artichoke hearts and sun-dried tomatoes in hand. A single coin escapes her change purse, bounces down the counter, coming to a rolling stop at my feet. It's a dime.

I stop in the office of my friend. She has a dime sitting on her immaculate desktop. "Where'd the dime come from?" I ask. "Oh, I don't know," she says. "I just found it on the floor of the closet."

Athens, Greece. 6:00 A.M., I'm the first one to be picked up by the tour bus that will take me to Delphi, the dwelling place of Apollo, considered by Greeks to be the center of the earth.

The bus is spotless, just cleaned. I move from seat to seat, trying to decide what will be the best view. I have so many choices! When I finally settle on my third choice, the tenth row from the front, right side, I put my purse on the floor, and there beside it—oh come on now, that's just showing off—one Euro ten-cent coin!

A few years ago, long after my father's death, while I was home visiting, my mother was going through her cassette tapes. She was looking for an empty tape so she could dub some music she liked for me. All the cassette tapes were unmarked, so she had to put each one into the tape player and listen to find out what it contained.

This is how we came upon a recording of the Statler Brothers singing "Flowers on the Wall," with my father's voice somehow mixed in, singing a ghostly second tenor part. My mother let the tape run. We sat at the kitchen table, listening in amazement.

"Where did this come from?" I asked. He was at it again, making crazy harmony, winding his voice around all the other parts.

"I don't know," my mother said. "He used to sit in front of the stereo and play these records over and over."

I realized that he must have used the mini-microphone on the boom box to record himself singing along with the record. When I told my mother, we shook our heads and laughed. It was good to hear his reedy voice lifted up once again in song.

Do the dead ever leave us? Do they watch over us as we sleep? I had a dream about my father several months after he died. He was so frail, lying on a cot in an empty room, his skin was jaundiced. He could barely speak. His small chest rose and fell. I could see that just for him to breathe was an effort.

His face was bony, as he smiled at me. His teeth were brown and falling out. He had only a few stubborn wisps of hair springing from his scalp. I felt terrible, seeing the state he was in. He was always so careful about his appearance. Now he was disheveled and small enough to hold in my arms. I sat down beside his bed and started to cry.

"What's wrong?" he asked, in the tender voice I remembered from childhood.

"I never came back to see you," I confessed. "When you were sick in the hospital, I never told you that I love you."

He took a deep breath and rested his head against the pillow. He waved his hand in dismissal.

"Of course you did," he said. His voice was a thin breeze moving through an empty chest. *Of course you did.*

EPILOGUE:
SUSTAINABLE AGRICULTURE:
The Farmer's Daughter Revisited

A traveling salesman is driving alone late at night.
He loses his way on a back road and knocks on a
farmer's door. He asks for a place to sleep.

—*Opening Lines to all Farmer's Daughter Jokes*

She waits, as all farmers' daughters must, in her bedroom at
the top of the wooden staircase, along the balustrade, down
the creaky hallway to the right. The light from her window
glows golden through lace curtains and spreads like a beacon
across the tilled fields, the thick black furrows and hundreds
of acres belonging only to the farmer that roll in waves
around the farmhouse.

It's important to know that the farmer's daughter is beautiful, that her beauty is like the sound of one hand clapping,
not in the forest, but in a cornfield or a wheat field where she
goes during the lonely days to spin in the ripeness, oblivious

of her beauty, which is the same oblivious corn-fed beauty and the same oblivious wheat field her mother spun in.

The traveling salesman is out there in the darkness, driving lost along the section lines, his product samples shuddering in the back seat with each washboard rut. He squints and downshifts. He rubs the windshield with the ragged sleeve of his suit coat and drives on, road-weary and blind, going deeper into the dark, rural night.

This must be the middle of nowhere, the traveling salesman thinks, the place of alien corn where the locals are friendly but suspicious, where the pitchforks are menacing.

His maps lie unconsulted and twisted in fat folds at his feet. Across many miles and states, his product samples for hybrid corn or aluminum siding, wire brushes or miraculous cleaning solutions, shift and sway, bristle and slosh in the back seat behind him.

One thing about the traveling salesman—he's good at neither travel nor sales. He never displays the products or demonstrates them to anyone. They ride in the back of the Buick like closely-held government secrets. He inherited this job from his father, who was retiring after thirty years of service, who was talkative and back-slapping, a natural salesman. This traveling salesman, the son, is reticent and inward, a shy homebody.

Down the gravel road and to the left, the farmer sits inside the farmhouse at his kitchen table, where all farmers must sit at the end of the day. He wears a clean white T-shirt and overalls. The bronze OshKosh buckles shine on his thick chest. The chores are finished, the cows are milked, the straw is spread.

He is busy now, reloading the shotgun shells he has emptied while shooting clay pigeons or chasing vermin from the yard. Whatever dares to enter the farmer's yard—fox, skunk, traveling salesmen—could come to know the experienced end of the farmer's shotgun. Maybe. Maybe not. His neck is red and leathery from driving the tractor all day in the sun, but he is no redneck. He has many fertile, rolling acres to defend; he must remain vigilant.

A cone of light shines over his bent head as he sits at the kitchen table weighing gunpowder on a scale, packing the wad of buckshot into the spent hulls. The small rounded BBs run down a funnel into the long, empty cartridge. He packs the shot tighter with his blunt thumb, then places the cartridge in the reloader, which compresses the wad and crimps the ends.

When finished, he lines up the shotgun shells, brass caps down, on the kitchen table. They gather in neat ranks like corn rows or like grain silos. The farmer is a farmer, after all; he must arrange things in rows.

Outside, a calm, green evening unfolds. The spring air is crisp and cool with a dewy edge. The vapor light buzzes to life, shining a megaphone of brightness onto the farmyard. Moths and mosquitoes and fireflies circle and rise, driven toward the sudden light.

Upstairs in her bedroom, the farmer's daughter reclines on her four-poster bed reading a book, her head propped against a pillow. Her long hair spreads, silky as a spider web, around her.

For the record, she is not busty or pig-tailed or wearing a checkered cotton shirt cross-tied at the navel. She lies on the bed, fresh from a shower wearing an oversized Rolling Stones T-shirt, her long legs crossed. As she reads, she bobs a delicate foot—her only sign of impatience.

The knock on the farmer's front door, when it comes, is not expected nor a surprise. It is neither too loud, nor too soft. It is just right. The farmer rises from his chair and turns on the porch light. Through the window he sees the young face of the traveling salesman—the wavy brown hair, the gaunt features, the dark worried eyes.

"Sorry to bother you so late," the salesman says when the door opens, his hat brim shifting in his large hands. The salesman glances into the lighted kitchen, sees the neat row of shotgun shells lined up on the table. He notes the presence of the polished Winchester with its two holes like nostrils propped on its wooden stock in the corner.

"I'm driving and I'm lost," the traveling salesman says to the farmer, swallowing hard, finding the words almost against his will. "And I'm wondering if I could trouble you for a place to sleep?"

The farmer wonders, could this be *his* traveling salesman? He notes the height of the boy—almost six feet—and the solid width of his shoulders, although thin under his dark suit. The farmer knows this is his moment; everything depends on his answer. Should he say, "We're a little tight on space, since the hired hand's sleeping in the spare room," as other farmers have said in the past? Should he offer to let the traveling salesman sleep in the barn? Not in this day and age.

The farmer shifts in the doorway and considers. "You'll have to share a room with my daughter," he finally relents, understanding that this is the only answer a farmer can give in response to a traveling salesman's request for a place to sleep.

Then he adds, significantly, "But don't you dare touch her."

Why is there never a farmer's wife in the story? Why never a farmer's son? The failure to produce sons is what drove the farmer's wife finally away—all those scowls from her husband in the pew on Sunday when the sermon turned to the subject of being fruitful and multiplying the earth.

The farmer's wife is now a waitress in Topeka or St. Paul where she dates a beefy, amorous truck driver who only comes around on the weekends. This suits the farmer's wife just fine. She likes having her weekdays to herself.

The hired hand, Hans or Ole, is indeed upstairs in the spare bedroom, perhaps whittling a long stick into a sharp point or lying on his bed reading *Popular Mechanics*. He has large fumbling hands, and cowlicks, and a toothy guffaw that bursts out of him when nothing especially funny has been said. In the beginning, the farmer had designs for the hired hand—perhaps a conjugal union with his daughter—but that was before he realized that the boy is no good with animals and not remotely interested in things that grow.

The hired hand is happiest when something on the farm breaks—when the baler stops twining, or the John Deere's engine stalls in the middle of a field, or a plow disk shatters against a buried boulder. His enthusiasm at these moments infuriates the farmer, who only keeps the hired hand around now because he's an ox with heavy loads and a genius with equipment. The hired hand is saving money to attend auto mechanic school in the fall at the nearby community college, although the farmer does not know this.

The farmer's daughter hears the traveling salesman coming through the house a long way off—his small leather suitcase bumping against the balusters, the footsteps creaking slowly along the dark upstairs hallway. She rises, leaving her book open, face down, on the bed. She knows she only has a few minutes.

She switches off the overhead light and clicks on the blacklight. The room goes dark, then a buzzing violet phosphorescence rises in the room. Ghostly letters emerge from posters on the wall announcing rock concerts she has not been able to attend—Woodstock, Monterey, Altamont. Her white teeth and her white Rolling Stones T-shirt with the wild red lips and tongue light up in the darkness.

She turns to face her record collection stacked tall in milk crates along the wall. She thumbs through and finds the album she wants—*Physical Graffiti*. She twirls the vinyl between her fingers, centers the record on the turntable, and searches for track six, "Kashmir." The needle settles with a scratch into the groove just as she hears the first timid knock.

"Come in," she sings. She plops down on her bed and picks up her book. From the speakers, the guitars crunch out the ascending chords. The door creaks open. The traveling salesman fills the doorway—worn black suit, long arms, shabby leather suitcase. The singer's voice goes "Ah, Ah."

"Don't tell me. Let me guess," the farmer's daughter says from behind her book, pretending not to look at the traveling salesman. "Lost on a country road." She adjusts the pillow behind her head. "Needed a place to sleep."

She thumbs through the pages of her book—Martin Heidegger's *Being and Time*—trying to recall the last part she read, something about the mystery and arbitrariness of what and where and whom one is born.

"Yes, I'm afraid so," the traveling salesman says with resignation. "That's exactly what happened." He moves into the dark room and drops his suitcase. The bedroom is made small by his height. He takes off his jacket. The wide shoulders of his white shirt glow in the black light.

As he bends to click open the latches of his suitcase, the farmer's daughter cranes her neck to see the shape and size of the salesman's hands, to note the way his fingers negotiate surfaces. The farmer's daughter has a thing about hands—she could never love a man unless she first loved his hands.

"Well, okay," she concedes, seeing enough. She pats the empty side of the bed. "I guess we're in this together."

The farmer's daughter leans over and opens a small drawer by her bedside table. From it, she draws out a baggie containing many long, robust twists of green-gold marijuana buds with auburn filaments shot through them. "No sense in making it hard on each other," she says.

The traveling salesman stares, incredulous, at the farmer's daughter. "You can get that stuff, out here?" He means to say, "in the middle of nowhere," but stops himself. He removes his size eleven shoes and drops them with a loud thump on the wood floor. In the room below, the farmer, lying in bed reading *True Crime* mysteries, takes note of this sound.

The farmer's daughter pulls two Zigzags from the slim white pack and licks a gluey edge. She affixes it to the other Zigzag with her forefinger and fans the paper in the air. "For your information," she says, bunching the weed in the paper crease and rolling up the joint in one quick swipe, "there's more than hard durham wheat growing on the north forty." She licks the glue, twists together the ends, and smooths out the edges of the paper with her tongue.

"But don't you dare tell my father," she adds smiling sideways at the traveling salesman as she flicks her lighter. The joint's tip flares in the black light. She inhales deeply, bringing the cherry to a bright glow, then, holding her breath, she hands the joint to the traveling salesman. He takes it between his fingers, brings the paper to his lips, and inhales deeply. The farmer's daughter exhales, a blue smoke filling the space between them. They smile at each other as the sweet mustiness fills the room.

At that moment, there's a loud knock on the bedroom door. It's a knock made by a big hairy-knuckled fist attached to a big beefy arm. The traveling salesman glances at the farmer's daughter in alarm. He rises to his feet, the smoldering roach between his fingers. Another knock comes. The door shakes on its hinges. A silence follows.

"I'm *okay*," the farmer's daughter yells impatiently in the direction of the closed door and slaps her hand on the bedspread.

Now the voice of the hired hand barks back through the door frame. "I'm supposed to keep an eye out for anything funny." It's the hired hand's only spoken line and his one assigned task—to watch for signs of hanky-panky.

"Well, there's nothing funny going on here," the farmer's daughter answers. She rolls her eyes at the traveling salesman.

The hired hand listens at the doorway for a moment, then retreats down the hallway to his room. He has heard electric guitar music, and he will report it to the farmer in the morning. He believes he smelled incense burning.

"I thought he'd never leave," the farmer's daughter says when the hired hand's footsteps disappear. She turns and switches off the blacklight. Small bits of moonlight filter through the curtain replacing the darkness.

"Now where were we?" she says, pulling the traveling salesman closer. She reaches for his face, begins to trace his worn and furrowed brow, the tired hollows of his eyes.

"There, there," she says. She brings her lips to his cheek, tastes the oily softness of his skin. "There, there," she says in the darkness, her hands mapping his sinewy curves and ridges, which unravel and let loose their exhaustion as her fingers travel over them.

The hours that follow are a tangle of sheets and limbs, of shifts, adjustments, and accommodations. To her surprise and her delight, she finds he follows simple instructions very well—*Yes, there; no, higher; harder; don't stop*—and he never tires of being told what to do. She decides to always value this in a man.

Toward morning, they settle into a rolling, dozing peacefulness. Between sleep and waking, they speak quietly of their disappointed fathers. She tells him she yearns to go to Paris or New York or Fargo. He speaks of his boyhood summers on his uncle's ranch in Wyoming—the smell of freshly mown hay, the satisfying heft of an alfalfa bale.

"Do you know how to work a stick shift?" she asks.

He props himself up on his elbow and chuckles, thinking it's some kind of kinky farmer's daughter sex talk. "I've been driving tractors since I was eight," he says.

She smiles widely, her back turned to him in the darkness.

In the earliest light of morning, the farmer's daughter slips out from under the traveling salesman's arm and gets dressed in the half light. She goes down the hallway to the bathroom to brush her teeth and wash her face. As she flosses, her beautiful corn-fed reflection stares back at her in the mirror.

The farmer and the hired hand, she knows, are already in the barn milking cows. On her way back to her bedroom, she sees the Winchester shotgun propped on its wooden stock in the hallway outside her door.

Inside she finds the traveling salesman sleeping peacefully on his side, the bed sheet pulled up around his waist. She lingers over him for a moment observing the softness of his features in sleep—his olive skin, his full lips, his delicate, well-shaped ears.

He is, she thinks, adorable in the early light; even his small drool on the pillow almost breaks her heart. She resists the urge to crawl back into bed with him, to feel the warmth of his skin, the weight of his arm circled around her.

Instead, she turns to her closet and retrieves her purse. She will take only a change of underwear and her small dial of pills. She rummages through the traveling salesman's suit coat draped over the back of the chair just where he left it. She finds the ring of car keys in the right-hand pocket.

Tiptoeing along the creaky hallway and down the wooden staircase, the farmer's daughter takes care not to wake the traveling salesman, who is actually awake, who has been awake since earliest light listening to the first morning call of birds. As the door closes, he rolls on his back, stretches his long legs out before him, and props his hands behind his head.

Through the open window, he can hear the cranky spark of the Buick's ignition as the farmer's daughter turns the key. The crunch of tires follows as he hears her put the car in gear and circle the gravel driveway. The traveling salesman smiles to himself, thinking that perhaps today, for all his trouble— the theft of the Buick, the irreplaceable loss of his product samples—the farmer will take him skeet shooting.

In the car, the girl turns right at the section line and bears down on the accelerator, leaving a long trail of dust in her wake. If she looked back now she would see the long winding driveway and a white farmhouse surrounded by neat out-buildings and tall cottonwoods that seem to stretch to the sky. If she looked back now, she would see her father in the doorway of the white barn, his hand raised to her in neither a fist nor a wave.

And so agriculture sustains itself and is sustained. Section lines weave and crisscross at every turning. Traveling salesmen must be lost before they can be found. Hired hands secretly wish to be mechanics. Loaded shotguns are propped against doorways but are never fired.

Farmers do not mean to be so possessive; they're just punctuated that way. And farmer's daughters must struggle against the powerful apostrophes of their fathers. They must drive away some early spring morning, hands planted firmly on the wheel, convinced they will never look back.

ACKNOWLEDGMENTS

Special thanks to the editors of the following journals in which some of these chapters originally appeared, sometimes in different forms: *Arts and Letters: Journal of Contemporary Culture, Brevity, Crab Orchard Review, Creative Nonfiction, Flyway: A Literary Review, Hayden's Ferry Review, Mid-American Review, New Letters, North Dakota Quarterly, Red Weather, Sub-Terrain, South Dakota Review, The Sun Magazine.*

"To Kill a Deer" was reprinted in *Dutiful Daughters: Reflecting on Our Parents as They Grow Old,* edited by Jean Gould (Seattle, Washington: Seal Press, 1999). "Things Not Seen in a Rearview Mirror" was reprinted in *Pushcart Prize Anthology XXVI: Best of the Small Presses* (New York: Pushcart Press, 2001).

First thanks go to the Department of English and the College of Liberal Arts and Sciences at Iowa State University, who have sustained me with research grants that allowed me to complete this work. A special thanks to the Iowa Arts Council, the Ragdale Foundation, the Ucross Foundation, the Pearl Hogrefe Fellowship, the Bread Loaf

Writers' Conference, the Sewanee Writers' Conference, and the Pirate's Alley Faulkner Society for their support. I'm especially grateful to the following editors who first read and published these evolving chapters: Robert Stewart and James McKinley at *New Letters,* William Borden and Robert Lewis at *North Dakota Quarterly,* Stephen Pett at *Flyway: A Literary Review,* Jon Tribble and Allison Joseph at *Crab Orchard Review,* Karen Babine and Michael Czyzniejewski at *Mid-American Review,* Dinty Moore at *Brevity,* and Martin Lammon at *Arts and Letters: Journal of Contemporary Culture.*

Special thanks go to Susan Dingle at the North Dakota State Historical Library and Michael Miller at the North Dakota State University Library. Thanks also to Mark Gonzalez at the North Dakota State Geological Survey; Allan C. Ashworth and Gary K. Clambey at North Dakota State University; and Zora Zimmerman, Joe-Ann McCoy, and James T. Andrews at Iowa State University. Any misinterpretation of the rich research they pointed me to is solely my responsibility.

Thanks to my colleague, Neil Nakadate, for his literary analysis of farmer's daughter jokes, and to David Arnason for his revisionist fairy tale "Girl and Wolf," which served as an inspiring template for my revision of the farmer's daughter's fate. A special thanks to Philip Bryant, Barbara Crow, Roger Gipple, Sheryl St. Germain, and Lew Marquardt, (my second cousin, once removed), for their enthusiastic responses to early drafts. Thanks also to Dona Reeves-Marquardt, for offering her expertise on the tricky German-Russian dialect.

I'm grateful to my friends at Minnesota State University–Moorhead, especially Mark Vinz and Thom Tammaro, who edited an important anthology of Midwestern literature, *Inheriting the Land.* Long overdue thanks to my first writing teacher, Mr. James Olig, who demanded impeccable sentences. I'm also grateful to the following teachers and mentors whose work continues to inspire me: Jane Smiley, Scott Russell Sanders, Patricia Hampl, Alan Davis, Mary Swander, and Ted Kooser.

Special thanks to my agent, Henry Dunow, who believed that there was a place in the world for this book; to Megan Husted who made a place in the world for it; to Carol Smith for her painstaking care with the manuscript; and to my editor, Amy Scheibe, who arrived at the exhausted end with fresh horses.

Finally, thanks to my family, especially my brother and my three sisters, with whom I share this story, and to my mother, who bravely continued to tell me stories even after she realized I was writing them down. My deepest love and gratitude go to them, and to Thomas, Adam, and Gabriel Rice, who see me through and make it all matter.

WORKS CITED

Arnason, David. "Girl and Wolf." *The Dragon & the Dry Goods Princess.* Winnipeg, Manitoba: Turnstone Press, 1995.

Ascherson, Neal. *Black Sea.* NY: Hill and Wang, Farrar, Straus and Giroux, 1995.

Castaneda, Carlos. *Journey to Ixtlan: The Lessons of Don Juan.* New York: Simon and Schuster, 1972.

Cather, Willa. *O Pioneers!* Boston: Houghton Mifflin, 1913.

Didion, Joan. *Slouching Towards Bethlehem.* NY: Dell Publishing, 1961.

Dittberner-Jax, Norita. *What They Always Were.* Minneapolis, MN: New Rivers Press, 1995.

Eliade, Mircea. *The Myth of the Eternal Return: Or, Cosmos and History.* Princeton: Princeton University Press, 1971.

Faulkner, William. *Absalom, Absalom!* NY: Modern Library, 1951.

Frazer, James George. *The Golden Bough: A Study in Magic and Religion.* NY: Macmillan, 1958.

Hampl, Patricia. *A Romantic Education.* Boston: Houghton Mifflin Company, 1981.

Jackson, Robert B., William T. Pockman, and William A. Hoffman. "The Structure and Function of Root Systems." *Handbook of Functional Plant Ecology.* Eds. Francisco I Pugnaire and Fernando Valladares. NY: M. Dekker, 1999.

Jackson, Wes. *Becoming Native to this Place.* Washington, DC: Counterpoint Press, 1996.

Leonard, A. G. *The Geology and Resources of North Dakota.* Grand Forks, ND: University of North Dakota, 1930.

Lowinsky, Naomi Ruth. "Mother of Mothers: The Power of the Grandmother in the Female Psyche." *To Be a Woman: The Birth of the Conscious Feminine.* Ed. Connie Zweig. Los Angeles: Jeremy P. Tarcher, Inc., 1990.

Manning, Richard. *Grassland: The History, Biology, Politics, and Promise of the American Prairie.* New York: Penguin Books, 1997.

Marquart, Debra. "I Am Upstairs, Trying to Be Quiet." *Everything's a Verb.* Minneapolis, MN: New Rivers Press, 1995.

Marquart, Debra. "Smokes." *The Hunger Bone: Rock & Roll Stories.* Minneapolis, MN: New Rivers Press, 2001.

Rölvaag, Ole. *Giants in the Earth: A Saga of the Prairie.* NY: Harper Collins, 1927.

Sanders, Scott Russell. "After the Flood." *Townships.* Ed. Michael Martone. Iowa City, IA: University of Iowa Press, 1992.

Stegner, Wallace. *Beyond the Hundredth Meridian: John Wesley Powell and the Second Opening of the West.* New York: Penguin Books, 1992.

Theweleit, Klaus. *Male Fantasies. Vol. 1: Women, Floods, Bodies, History.* Minneapolis, MN: University of Minnesota Press, 1987.

Welk, Lawrence. *Wunnerful, Wunnerful: The Autobiography of Lawrence Welk.* New York: Prentice Hall, 1971.

Wheeler, Sylvia Griffith. "Earthlings." *Inheriting the Land: Contemporary Voices from the Midwest.* Ed. Mark Vinz and Thom Tammaro. Minneapolis, MN: University of Minnesota Press, 1993.